Mathematics for CS/IT
Linear Algebra Concepts with Real Life Applications

Table of Contents

Basics of Linear Algebra

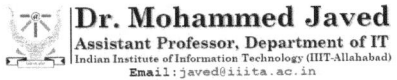 **Dr. Mohammed Javed**
Assistant Professor, Department of IT
Indian Institute of Information Technology (IIIT-Allahabad)
Email: javed@iiita.ac.in

Video Lectures for the book contents are available at

https://www.youtube.com/channel/UCjuoLDHnvDBenbBdFD3pQUw

Content Reference Book :
Introduction to Linear Algebra by Gilbert Strang, MIT

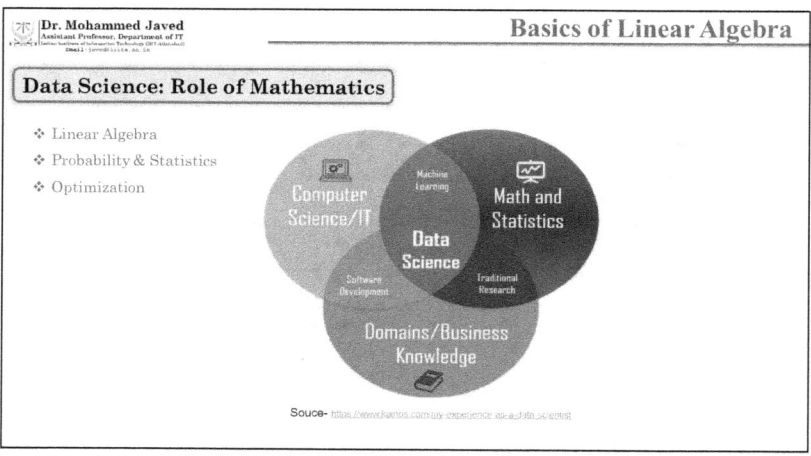

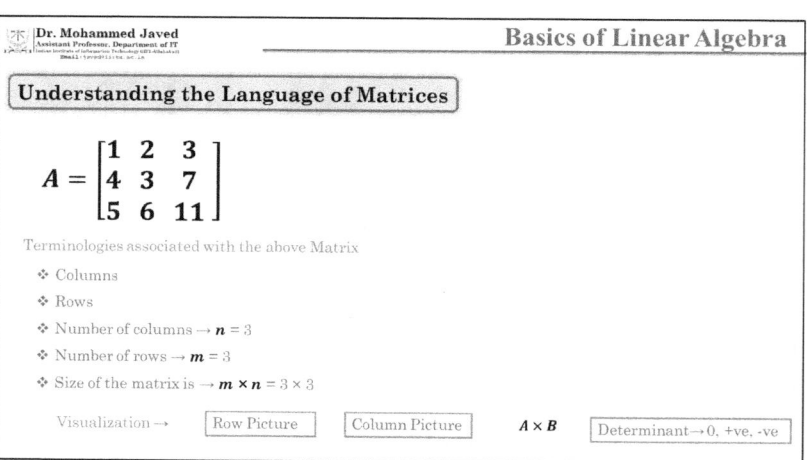

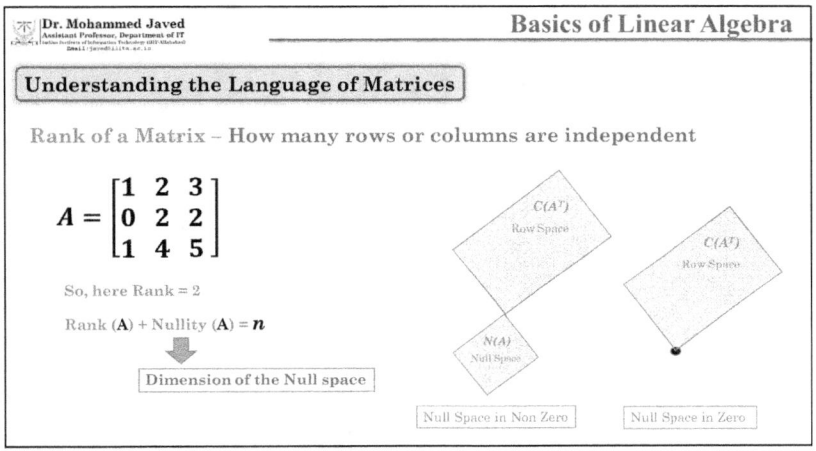

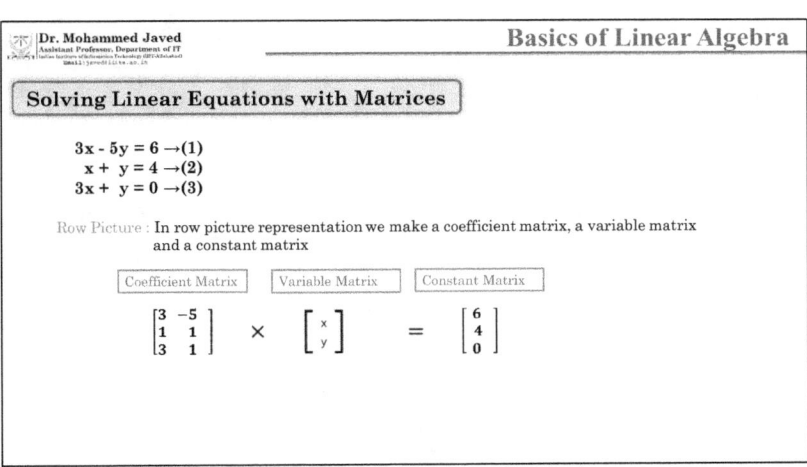

Dr. Mohammed Javed
Assistant Professor, Department of IT
Indian Institute of Information Technology (IIT-Allahabad)
Email : javed@iiita.ac.in

Basics of Linear Algebra

Solving Linear Equations with Matrices

Row Picture : In row picture representation we make a coefficient matrix, a variable matrix and a constant matrix

Coefficient Matrix   Variable Matrix   Constant Matrix

$$\begin{bmatrix} 3 & -5 \\ 1 & 1 \\ 3 & 1 \end{bmatrix} \times \begin{bmatrix} x \\ y \end{bmatrix} = \begin{bmatrix} 6 \\ 4 \\ 0 \end{bmatrix}$$

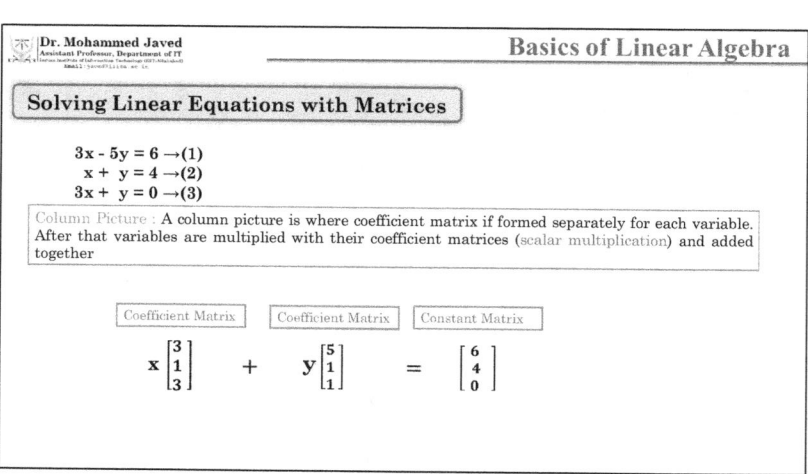

❖ To find solution of system of linear equations from Row picture

❖ We look at graph and see if there is any one point of intersection for all the lines.

❖ That point is called solution for the system of equations.

❖ If there is no common point, then there is no solution for the system of equations

---

Dr. Mohammed Javed
Assistant Professor, Department of IT
Indian Institute of Information Technology (IIT-Allahabad)
Email : javed@iiita.ac.in

Basics of Linear Algebra

Solving Linear Equations with Matrices

$3x - 5y = 6 \rightarrow (1)$
$x + y = 4 \rightarrow (2)$
$3x + y = 0 \rightarrow (3)$

Column Picture : A column picture is where coefficient matrix if formed separately for each variable. After that variables are multiplied with their coefficient matrices (scalar multiplication) and added together

Coefficient Matrix   Coefficient Matrix   Constant Matrix

$$x \begin{bmatrix} 3 \\ 1 \\ 3 \end{bmatrix} + y \begin{bmatrix} 5 \\ 1 \\ 1 \end{bmatrix} = \begin{bmatrix} 6 \\ 4 \\ 0 \end{bmatrix}$$

Dr. Mohammed Javed
Assistant Professor, Department of IT
Indian Institute of Information Technology (IIIT-Allahabad)
Email : javed@iiita.ac.in

Basics of Linear Algebra

Solving Linear Equations with Matrices

Column Picture : A column picture is where coefficient matrix if formed separately for each variable. After that variables are multiplied with their coefficient matrices (scalar multiplication) and added together

| Coefficient Matrix | Coefficient Matrix | Constant Matrix |

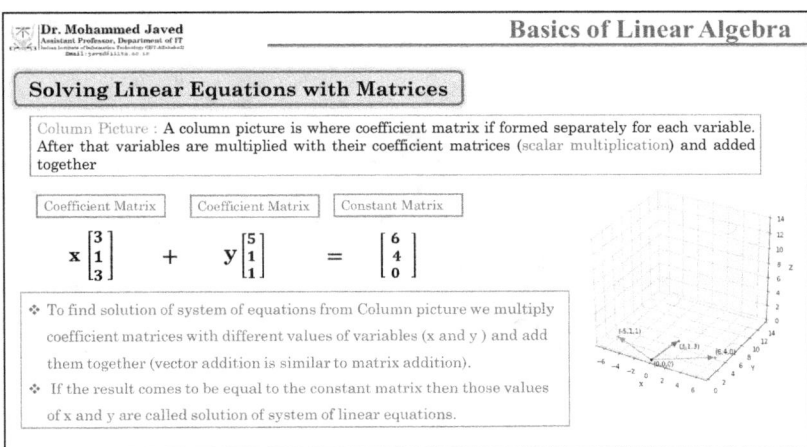

$$x \begin{bmatrix} 3 \\ 1 \\ 3 \end{bmatrix} + y \begin{bmatrix} 5 \\ 1 \\ 1 \end{bmatrix} = \begin{bmatrix} 6 \\ 4 \\ 0 \end{bmatrix}$$

❖ To find solution of system of equations from Column picture we multiply coefficient matrices with different values of variables (x and y) and add them together (vector addition is similar to matrix addition).

❖ If the result comes to be equal to the constant matrix then those values of x and y are called solution of system of linear equations.

Dr. Mohammed Javed
Assistant Professor, Department of IT
Indian Institute of Information Technology (IIIT-Allahabad)
Email : javed@iiita.ac.in

Basics of Linear Algebra

Understanding the Language of Matrices

$$Ax = \begin{bmatrix} 1 & 2 & 3 \\ 4 & 3 & 7 \\ 5 & 6 & 11 \end{bmatrix} \begin{bmatrix} x_1 \\ x_2 \\ x_3 \end{bmatrix}$$

| Row wise |
| Column wise |

Column Picture

$$Ax = x_1 \begin{bmatrix} 1 \\ 4 \\ 5 \end{bmatrix} + x_2 \begin{bmatrix} 2 \\ 3 \\ 6 \end{bmatrix} + x_3 \begin{bmatrix} 3 \\ 7 \\ 11 \end{bmatrix} = b$$

❖ They are vectors (Advantage)
❖ Right side says that Ax is a linear combination of the columns
❖ This is the fundamental idea of Linear Algebra

Linear Algebra Concepts with Real Life
Applications

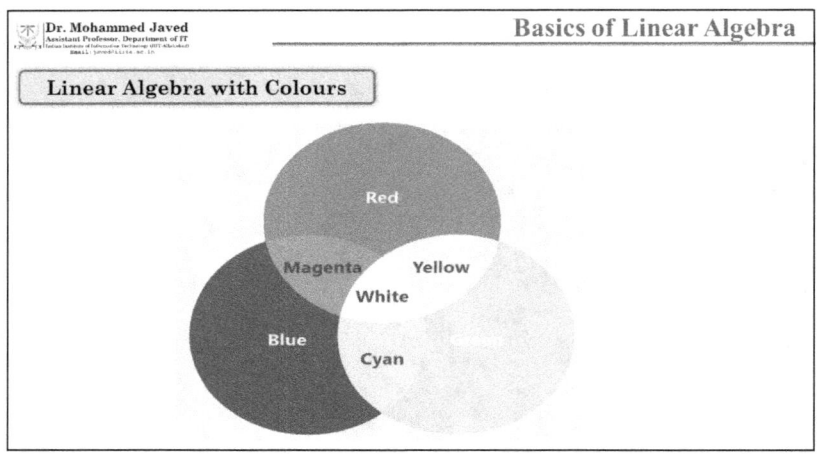

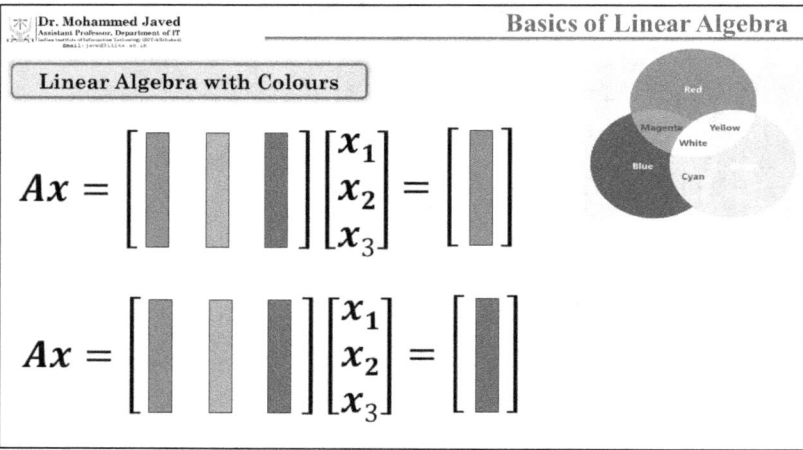

Linear Algebra Concepts with Real Life
Applications

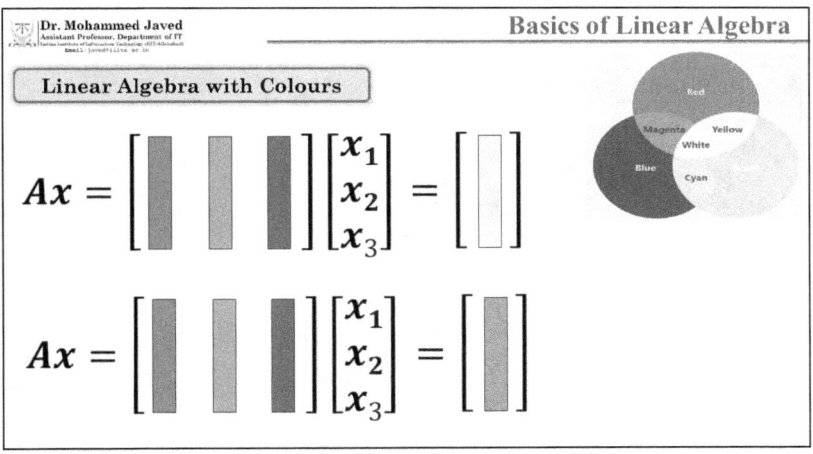

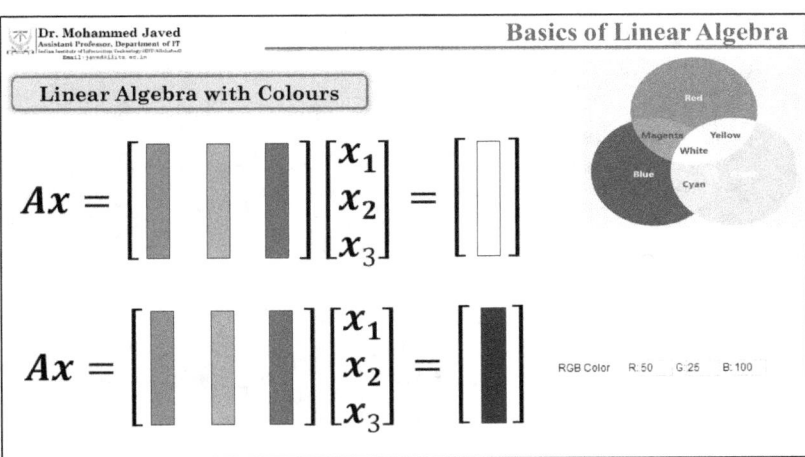

Dr. Mohammed Javed
Assistant Professor, Department of IT
Indian Institute of Information Technology (IIIT-Allahabad)
Email: javed@iiita.ac.in

Basics of Linear Algebra

Column Space and Basis of a Matrix

- ❖ Linear combinations of the columns is equal to column space of the matrix
- ❖ Basis of a Column Space is the critical idea of Linear algebra
- ❖ A Basis is a bunch of vectors, specific vectors in the space
- ❖ There are many basis in a matrix for a column space
- ❖ Standard basis for a matrix is the identity matrix

$$\begin{bmatrix} 1 & 0 & 0 \\ 0 & 1 & 0 \\ 0 & 0 & 1 \end{bmatrix}$$

Key Properties of a Basis

- ❖ They are Linearly Independent
- ❖ They span the entire space of the matrix

Dr. Mohammed Javed
Assistant Professor, Department of IT
Indian Institute of Information Technology (IIIT-Allahabad)
Email: javed@iiita.ac.in

Basics of Linear Algebra

Factorization of Matrix

- ❖ Matrix Factorization is the key in exploring Data Science
- ❖ They help in breaking the Big Matrix into Smaller Pieces easy to comprehend and analyse
- ❖ There are many matrix factorization techniques, here we show $A = CR$
- ❖ Row basis (row space) times the column basis (column space)

$$A = \begin{bmatrix} 1 & 2 & 3 \\ 4 & 3 & 7 \\ 5 & 6 & 11 \end{bmatrix}$$ So, here Rank = 2

$$A = CR = \begin{bmatrix} 1 & 2 \\ 4 & 3 \\ 5 & 6 \end{bmatrix} \begin{bmatrix} 1 & 0 & 1 \\ 0 & 1 & 1 \end{bmatrix}$$

Dr. Mohammed Javed
Assistant Professor, Department of IT
Indian Institute of Information Technology (IIIT-Allahabad)
Email: javed@iiita.ac.in

Basics of Linear Algebra

Factorization of Matrix

❖ Matrix Factorization is the key in exploring Data Science
❖ They help in breaking the Big Matrix into Smaller Pieces easy to comprehend and analyse
❖ There are many matrix factorization techniques

❑ Elimination Method $A = LU$

❑ Gram Schmidt Method* $A = QR$

❑ SVD $A = U \Sigma V^T$

*Q is orthogonal Matrix and R is Upper Triangular Matrix

Linear Transformation

Dr. Mohammed Javed
Assistant Professor, Department of IT
Indian Institute of Information Technology (IIIT-Allahabad)
Email: javed@iiita.ac.in

Video Lectures for the book contents are available at

https://www.youtube.com/channel/UCjuoLDHnvDBenbBdFD3pQUw

Content Reference Book :
Introduction to Linear Algebra by Gilbert Strang, MIT

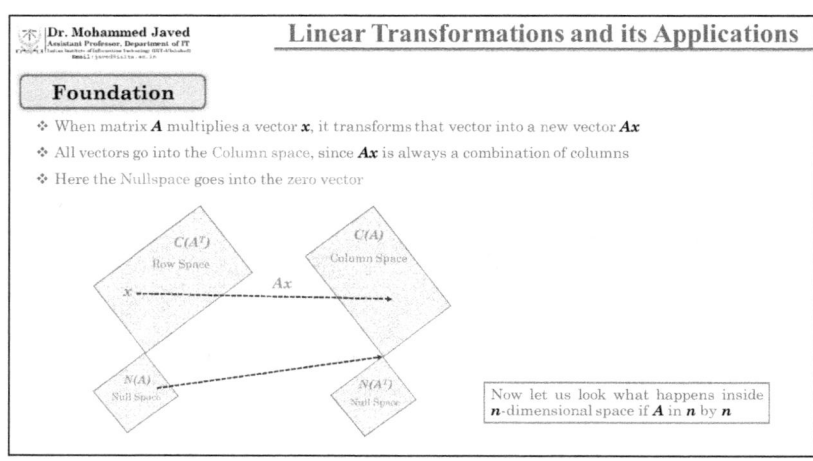

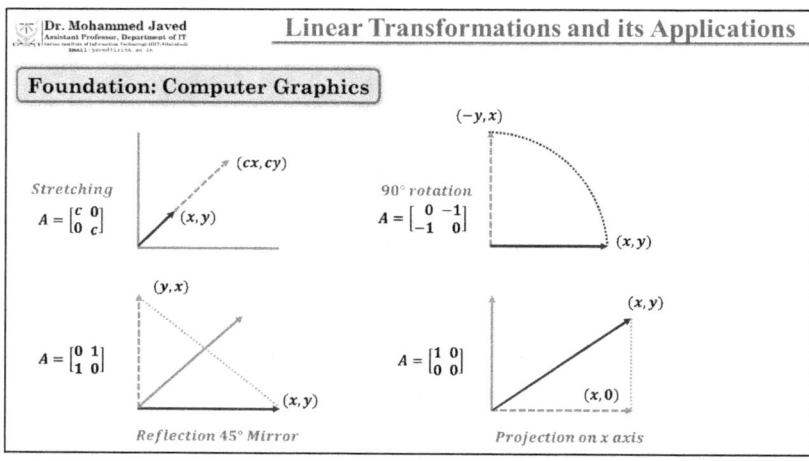

Dr. Mohammed Javed
Assistant Professor, Department of IT
Indian Institute of Information Technology (IIIT-Allahabad)
Email: javed@iiita.ac.in

Linear Transformations and its Applications

Foundation: Linear Algebra

❖ Let us take the case of $Av = v$ $Av = \begin{bmatrix} a & c \\ b & d \end{bmatrix}\begin{bmatrix} 2 \\ 3 \end{bmatrix} = \begin{bmatrix} 2 \\ 3 \end{bmatrix} \rightarrow A = \begin{bmatrix} 1 & 0 \\ 0 & 1 \end{bmatrix}$

❖ Let us take the case of $Av = w$ $Av = \begin{bmatrix} a & c \\ b & d \end{bmatrix}\begin{bmatrix} 2 \\ 3 \end{bmatrix} = \begin{bmatrix} 4 \\ 6 \end{bmatrix} \rightarrow A = \begin{bmatrix} 2 & 0 \\ 0 & 2 \end{bmatrix}$

❖ When the basis are same A is identity

❖ When v and w change the A changes

> Change of basis produces different A

Dr. Mohammed Javed
Assistant Professor, Department of IT
Indian Institute of Information Technology (IIIT-Allahabad)
Email: javed@iiita.ac.in

Linear Transformations and its Applications

The Idea of Linear Transformation

❖ When a matrix A multiplies a vector v, it transforms v into another vector Av
❖ A transformation T follows the same idea as a function like x goes in $f(x)$ comes out
❖ The deeper goal is to see all the v's at once
❖ We are transforming the whole space V when we multiply every v by A
❖ Matrix multiplication $T(v) = Av$ gives a linear transformation

A transformation T assigns an output $T(v)$ to each input vector v in V.

The transformation in linear if it meets these requirements for all v and w:

(a) $T(v+w) = T(v)+T(w)$ (b) $T(cv) = cT(v)$ for all c

> Combined: Linear Transformation is $T(cv + dw)$ must equal $cT(v) + dT(w)$

Dr. Mohammed Javed
Assistant Professor, Department of IT
Indian Institute of Information Technology (IIT) Allahabad
Email: javed@iiita.ac.in

Linear Transformations and its Applications

Shift Operation is not linear

❖ Suppose T adds u_0 to every vector. Then $T(v) = v + u_0$ and $T(w) = w + u_0$

❖ Applying T to $v + w$ produces $v + w + u_0$, which is not same as $T(v) + T(w) = v + u_0 + w + u_0$

❖ Exception is when $u_0 = 0$

The Linear + Shift transformation $T(v) = Av + u_0$ is called affine

❖ Straight lines stay straight although T is not linear

❖ Edge parallelism is also maintained here

❖ Computer Graphics work with Affine Transformations to move images

Note: If the output involves Squares or Products or Lengths, v_1^2 or $v_1 v_2$ or $\|v\|$, then T is not linear

---

Dr. Mohammed Javed
Assistant Professor, Department of IT
Indian Institute of Information Technology (IIT) Allahabad
Email: javed@iiita.ac.in

Linear Transformations and its Applications

Length $T(v) = \|v\|$ is not linear

❖ For linearity we require (a) $\|v + w\| = \|v\| + \|w\|$ and (b) $\|cv\| = c\|v\|$ Both are False

Not (a): The sides of a triangle satisfy an inequality $\|v + w\| \leq \|v\| + \|w\|$

Not (b): The length $\|-v\|$ *is not* $-\|v\|$. For negative c we fail

Is Rotation Linear?

❖ Let T be a transformation that rotates every vector by $30°$

❖ The domain is the xy plane (all input vectors v), the range is also the xy plane (all rotated vectors $T(v)$)

❖ The sum of rotations $T(v) + T(w)$ is the same as the rotation $T(v + w)$

❖ The whole plane is turning together, in this linear transformation

Linear Algebra Concepts with Real Life
Applications

Dr. Mohammed Javed
Assistant Professor, Department of IT
Indian Institute of Information Technology (IIT-Allahabad)
Email: javed@iiita.ac.in

Linear Transformations and its Applications

Linear Transformation of Points

❖ Every point on the input line goes onto the output line

❖ Equally spaced points go to equally spaced points

❖ The middle point $u = \frac{1}{2}v + \frac{1}{2}w$ goes to $T(u) = \frac{1}{2}T(v) + \frac{1}{2}T(w)$

❖ The input triangle goes onto the output triangle

❖ Equally spaced points stay equally spaced

❖ Middle point $u = \frac{1}{3}(v_1 + v_2 + v_3)$ goes to $T(u) = \frac{1}{3}(T(v_1) + T(v_2) + T(v_3))$

The rule of linearity extends to combinations of three vectors to n vectors

---

Dr. Mohammed Javed
Assistant Professor, Department of IT
Indian Institute of Information Technology (IIT-Allahabad)
Email: javed@iiita.ac.in

Linear Transformations and its Applications

Range and Kernel of Transformations T

❖ Range of T = set of all outputs $T(v)$: range corresponds to column space (outputs of Av)

❖ Kernel of T = set of all inputs for which $T(v) = 0$): Kernel corresponds to Null space

❖ The Range is in the output space W and the kernel is in the input space V

Examples of Transformation:

❖ Project every 3-dimensional vector straight down onto the xy plane. Then $T(x,y,z) = (x,y,0)$ This projection is linear.

❖ Project every 3-dimensional vector onto the horizontal plane $z = 1$. The vector $v = (x, y, z)$ is transformed to $T(v) = (x, y, 1)$. This transformation is not linear. (it does not even transform $v = 0$ into $T(v) = 0$).

❖ Suppose A is an invertible matrix. The kernel of T is the zero vector; the range W equals the domain V. Another linear transformation is multiplication by A^{-1}. This is the inverse transformation T^{-1}, which brings every vector $T(v)$ back to v:

$$T^{-1}(T(v)) = v \text{ matches the matrix multiplication } A^{-1}(Av) = v$$

Dr. Mohammed Javed
Assistant Professor, Department of IT

Linear Transformations and its Applications

Linear Transformation of the Plane

Plot2d(A*H)

❖ When a 2×2 matrix multiplies all vectors in $\mathbf{R^2}$ we can watch how it acts.

❖ The house that has eleven endpoints. Those elven vectors are transformed into eleven vectors Av

❖ The columns of H are eleven corners of the house, which are multiplied by A to produce corners AH

$$H = \begin{bmatrix} -6 & -6 & -7 & 0 & 7 & 6 & 6 & -3 & -3 & 0 & 0 & -6 \\ -7 & 2 & 1 & 8 & 1 & 2 & -7 & -7 & -2 & -2 & -7 & -7 \end{bmatrix}$$

$A = \begin{bmatrix} 1 & 0 \\ 0 & 1 \end{bmatrix}$ $A = \begin{bmatrix} cos\,35° & -sin\,35° \\ sin\,35° & cos\,35° \end{bmatrix}$ $A = \begin{bmatrix} 0 & 1 \\ 1 & 0 \end{bmatrix}$ $A = \begin{bmatrix} 0.7 & 0.3 \\ 0.3 & 0.7 \end{bmatrix}$

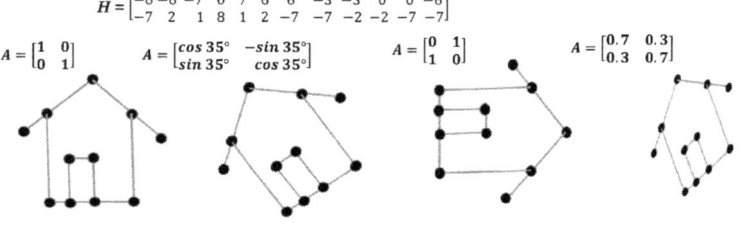

Dr. Mohammed Javed
Assistant Professor, Department of IT

Linear Transformations and its Applications

The Matrix of Linear Transformation

❖ For ordinary column vector, the input v is in $\mathbf{V = R^n}$ and the output $T(v)$ is in $\mathbf{W = R^m}$

❖ The matrix A for this transformation T will be m by n and choice of bases $\mathbf{V}$ and $\mathbf{W}$ will decide $\mathbf{A}$

❖ The standard basis vectors for $\mathbf{R^n}$ and $\mathbf{R^m}$ are the columns of I which leads to standard matrix $T(v) = Av$

❖ But there also other bases, so linear algebra aims to choose the bases that give the best matrix for T

❖ When $\mathbf{V}$ and $\mathbf{W}$ are not $\mathbf{R^n}$ and $\mathbf{R^m}$, they still have bases

❖ Each choice of bases will lead to a matrix for T

❖ When the input basis is different from the output basis, the matrix for $T(v) = v$ will not be an identity I

❖ It will be the change of basis matrix, like in case of JPEG

Dr. Mohammed Javed
Assistant Professor, Department of IT
Indian Institute of Information Technology (IIIT-Allahabad)
Email: javed@iiita.ac.in

Linear Transformations and its Applications

The Matrix of Linear Transformation

Example 1: $\mathbf{R^2 \to R^3}$

❖ Suppose T transforms basis vector $v_1 = (1, 0)$ to $T(v_1) = (2, 3, 4)$

❖ Suppose the second basis vector $v_2 = (0, 1)$ goes to $T(v_2) = (5, 5, 5)$

❖ If T is linear from $\mathbf{R^2}$ to $\mathbf{R^3}$, then the standard matrix is 3 by 2.

❖ Those outputs $T(v_1)$ and $T(v_2)$ go into the columns

$$A = \begin{bmatrix} 2 & 5 \\ 3 & 5 \\ 4 & 5 \end{bmatrix}$$

$T(v_1 + v_2) = T(v_1) + T(v_2)$ combines the columns

$$\begin{bmatrix} 2 & 5 \\ 3 & 5 \\ 4 & 5 \end{bmatrix} \begin{bmatrix} 1 \\ 1 \end{bmatrix} = \begin{bmatrix} 7 \\ 8 \\ 9 \end{bmatrix}$$

$$[A]\begin{bmatrix} 1 \\ 0 \end{bmatrix} = \begin{bmatrix} 2 \\ 3 \\ 4 \end{bmatrix} \qquad [A]\begin{bmatrix} 0 \\ 1 \end{bmatrix} = \begin{bmatrix} 5 \\ 5 \\ 5 \end{bmatrix}$$

$$[m \times n][2 \times 1] = [3 \times 1]$$

$$m = 3 \qquad n = 2$$

Dr. Mohammed Javed
Assistant Professor, Department of IT
Indian Institute of Information Technology (IIIT-Allahabad)
Email: javed@iiita.ac.in

Linear Transformations and its Applications

The Matrix of Linear Transformation

Example 2: **Derivative Matrix**

❖ The derivative of the functions $1, x, x^2, x^3$ are $0, 1, 2x, 3x^2$

❖ The inputs and outputs are functions

$$T(v) = \frac{dv}{dx} \qquad \text{Obeys the linearity rule} \qquad \frac{d}{dx}(cv + dw) = c\frac{dv}{dx} + d\frac{dw}{dx}$$

❖ The range of T is three dimensional subspace. The matrix will have rank $r = 3$

❖ The kernel is one dimensional.

❖ The sum $3 + 1 = 4$ is the dimension of the input space

❖ $r + (n - r) = n$ is the Fundamental Theorem of Linear Algebra

❖ Dimension of range + Dimension of kernel = Dimension of input space

Linear Algebra Concepts with Real Life
Applications

Dr. Mohammed Javed
Assistant Professor, Department of IT
Indian Institute of Information Technology (IIIT-Allahabad)
Email : javed@iiita.ac.in

Linear Transformations and its Applications

The Matrix of Linear Transformation

Example 2: **Derivative Matrix**

❖ The derivative of the functions *1, x, x², x³* are *0, 1, 2x, 3x²*

❖ The basis for **V** is *1, x, x², x³* and the basis for **W** is *1, x, x²*

❖ The derivate matrix *A* is 3 by 4

$$\begin{bmatrix} 0 & 1 & 0 & 0 \\ 0 & 0 & 2 & 0 \\ 0 & 0 & 0 & 3 \end{bmatrix} \begin{bmatrix} 1 \\ x \\ x^2 \\ x^3 \end{bmatrix} = \begin{bmatrix} 1 \\ 2x \\ 3x^2 \end{bmatrix}$$

$$A = \begin{bmatrix} 0 & 1 & 0 & 0 \\ 0 & 0 & 2 & 0 \\ 0 & 0 & 0 & 3 \end{bmatrix} = The\ matrix\ form\ of\ derivative\ T$$

Dr. Mohammed Javed
Assistant Professor, Department of IT
Indian Institute of Information Technology (IIIT-Allahabad)
Email : javed@iiita.ac.in

Linear Transformations and its Applications

The Matrix of Linear Transformation

Example 3: **Integral is the inverse of Derivative** – Fundamental Theorem of Calculus

❖ The transformation T^{-1} that takes the integral from 0 to x is linear.

❖ Applying T^{-1} to functions *1, x, x²* which are , w_1, w_2, w_3

Integration of T^{-1} $\quad \int_0^x 1\, dx = x \quad \int_0^x x\, dx = \frac{1}{2}x^2 \quad \int_0^x x^2\, dx = \frac{1}{3}x^3$

❖ By linearity, the integral of $w = B + Cx + Dx^2$ is

$$T^{-1}(w) = Bx + \frac{1}{2}Cx^2 + \frac{1}{3}Dx^3$$

❖ Integration takes **W** back to **V**

❖ The input space of T^{-1} is the quadratics, and the output space is the cubics

❖ The Integration matrix will be 4 by 3

Dr. Mohammed Javed
Assistant Professor, Department of IT
Indian Institute of Information Technology (IIIT-Allahabad)
Email: javed@iiita.ac.in

Linear Transformations and its Applications

The Matrix of Linear Transformation

Example 3: **Integral is the inverse of Derivative – Fundamental Theorem of Calculus**

❖ The matrix starts with $w = B + Cx + Dx^2$ and produces $0 + Bx + \frac{1}{2}Cx^2 + \frac{1}{3}Dx^3$

$$\begin{bmatrix} 0 & 0 & 0 \\ 1 & 0 & 0 \\ 0 & 1/2 & 0 \\ 0 & 0 & 1/3 \end{bmatrix} \begin{bmatrix} B \\ C \\ D \end{bmatrix} = \begin{bmatrix} 0 \\ B \\ \frac{1}{2}C \\ \frac{1}{3}D \end{bmatrix}$$

$$A = \begin{bmatrix} 0 & 0 & 0 \\ 1 & 0 & 0 \\ 0 & 1/2 & 0 \\ 0 & 0 & 1/3 \end{bmatrix} = The\ matrix\ form\ of\ Integral\ T^{-1}$$

Dr. Mohammed Javed
Assistant Professor, Department of IT
Indian Institute of Information Technology (IIIT-Allahabad)
Email: javed@iiita.ac.in

Linear Transformations and its Applications

Construction of the Matrix

❖ Suppose T transforms the space $\mathbf{V}$ (n-dimensional) to the space $\mathbf{W}$ (m-dimensional)

❖ $\mathbf{W}$ choose a basis $v_1, \ldots, v_n$ for $\mathbf{V}$ and we choose a basis $w_1, \ldots, w_m$ for $\mathbf{W}$

❖ The matrix will be m by n

❖ To find the first column of A, apply T to the first basis vector v_1

❖ The output $T(v_1)$ is in $\mathbf{W}$.

❖ $T(v_1)$ is a combination $a_{11}w_1 + \ldots + a_{m1}w_m$ of the output basis vector $\mathbf{W}$

❖ Those numbers $a_{11}, \ldots, a_{m1}$ go into the first column of A.

When T is the derivative and the first basis vector is 1, its derivative is $T(v_1) = 0$.
So for the derivative matrix, the first column of A was all Zero $\rightarrow$ **(0, 0, 0)**

For the integral, the basis function again was 1. Its integral is the second basis function x.
So the first column of Integral matrix was **(0, 1, 0, 0)**

Dr. Mohammed Javed
Assistant Professor, Department of IT   **Linear Transformations and its Applications**

Change of bases

❖ The matrix A tells us what T does,

❖ Every linear transformation from V to W can be converted to a matrix

❖ The matrix depends on the bases.

Example 4: If the bases change, T is the same but the matrix A is different

❖ Suppose we reorder the basis to $x, x_2, x_3, 1$ for the cubics in V

❖ Keep the original basis $1, x, x_2$ for the quadratics in W

❖ The derivative of the first basis vector $v_1 = x$ is the first basis vector $w_1 = 1$

$$A = \begin{bmatrix} 1 & 0 & 0 & 0 \\ 0 & 2 & 0 & 0 \\ 0 & 0 & 3 & 0 \end{bmatrix} = matrix\ for\ the\ derivative\ T\ when\ the\ bases\ change$$

Dr. Mohammed Javed
Assistant Professor, Department of IT   **Linear Transformations and its Applications**

Rotation as Transformation

Example 4: T rotates every vector by an angle θ. Here $V = W = R^2$. Find A ?

❖ The standard basis is $v_1 = (1,0)$ and $v_2 = (0,1)$

❖ To find A, apply T to those basis vectors.

❖ The first vector $(1,0)$ swings around to $(cos\ \theta, sin\ \theta)$. This equals $cos\ \theta$ times $(1,0) + sin\ \theta$ times $(0,1)$

❖ Therefore $cos\ \theta$ and $sin\ \theta$ go into the firs column of A

❖ For the second column, transform the second vector $(0,1)$, gets rotated by $(- sin\ \theta, cos\ \theta)$

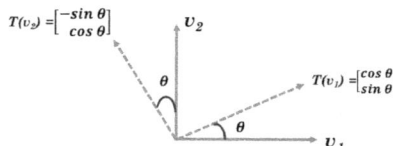

$$T(v_2) = \begin{bmatrix} -sin\ \theta \\ cos\ \theta \end{bmatrix}$$

$$T(v_1) = \begin{bmatrix} cos\ \theta \\ sin\ \theta \end{bmatrix}$$

Dr. Mohammed Javed
Assistant Professor, Department of IT
Indian Institute of Information Technology (IIIT) Allahabad
Email: javed@iiita.ac.in
Linear Transformations and its Applications

Projection as Transformation

Example 5: (Projection) **Suppose T projects every plane vector onto the 45° line. Find its matrix for two different choices of the basis. We will find two matrices.**

❖ The basis vector v_1 is along the **45°** line. It projects itself : $T(v_1) = v_1$

❖ The first column of A contains 1 and 0

❖ The second basis vector v2 is along the perpendicular line **135°**

❖ This basis vector projects to zero. So the second column of A contains 0 and 0

Projection $A = \begin{bmatrix} 1 & 0 \\ 0 & 0 \end{bmatrix}$ when V and W have the 45° and 135° basis

Dr. Mohammed Javed
Assistant Professor, Department of IT
Indian Institute of Information Technology (IIIT) Allahabad
Email: javed@iiita.ac.in
Linear Transformations and its Applications

Product AB matches Transformation TS

Example 5: (Projection) **Suppose T projects every plane vector onto the 45° line. Find its matrix for two different choices of the basis. We will find two matrices.**

❖ Now take the standard basis **(1,0)** and **(0,1)**.

❖ They project to $(\frac{1}{2}, \frac{1}{2})$ which gives the first column of A

❖ The other basis vector **(0,1)** also projects to $(\frac{1}{2}, \frac{1}{2})$.

❖ So the standard matrix for this projection is A:

Same Projection $A = \begin{bmatrix} \frac{1}{2} & \frac{1}{2} \\ \frac{1}{2} & \frac{1}{2} \end{bmatrix}$ for the standard basis

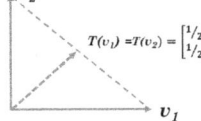

$T(v_1) = T(v_2) = \begin{bmatrix} 1/2 \\ 1/2 \end{bmatrix}$

❖ Both A's are projection matrices.

❖ If you square A it doesn't change.

❖ Projecting twice is the same as projecting once: $T^2 = T$ so $A^2 = A$

❖ The matrix for T^2 is A^2

 **Dr. Mohammed Javed**
Assistant Professor, Department of IT
Indian Institute of Information Technology (IIIT-Allahabad)
Email : javed@iiita.ac.in

Linear Transformations and its Applications

Product AB matches Transformation TS

❖ Matrix multiplication gives the correct matrix **AB** to represent **TS**

❖ Product of transformations matches product of matrices

Example 6: If **S** rotates the plane by **θ** and **T** also rotates by **θ**. Then TS rotates by **2θ** . This transformation T^2 corresponds to the rotation matrix A^2 through **2θ**

$$T = S \qquad A = B \qquad T^2 = rotation\ by\ 2\theta \qquad A^2 = \begin{bmatrix} cos\ 2\theta & -Sin\ 2\theta \\ sin\ 2\theta & cos\ 2\theta \end{bmatrix}$$

$$A \times A = \begin{bmatrix} cos\ \theta & -Sin\ \theta \\ sin\ \theta & cos\ \theta \end{bmatrix}\begin{bmatrix} cos\ \theta & -Sin\ \theta \\ sin\ \theta & cos\ \theta \end{bmatrix} = \begin{bmatrix} cos^2\ \theta - sin^2\ \theta & -2\ sin\ \theta\ cos\ \theta \\ 2\ sin\ \theta\ cos\ \theta & cos^2\ \theta - sin^2\ \theta \end{bmatrix} = \begin{bmatrix} cos\ 2\theta & -Sin\ 2\theta \\ sin\ 2\theta & cos\ 2\theta \end{bmatrix}$$

Example 7: **T** took derivative and **S** took integral. The transformation **TS** is the identity but not **ST**. Therefore **AB** is the identity matrix but not **BA**

$$AB = \begin{bmatrix} 0 & 1 & 0 & 0 \\ 0 & 0 & 2 & 0 \\ 0 & 0 & 0 & 3 \end{bmatrix}\begin{bmatrix} 0 & 0 & 0 \\ 1 & 0 & 0 \\ 0 & 1/2 & 0 \\ 0 & 0 & 1/3 \end{bmatrix} = I \qquad BA = \begin{bmatrix} 0 & 0 & 0 & 0 \\ 0 & 1 & 0 & 0 \\ 0 & 0 & 1 & 0 \\ 0 & 0 & 0 & 1 \end{bmatrix}$$

Discrete Wavelet Transform

 **Dr. Mohammed Javed**
Assistant Professor, Department of IT
Indian Institute of Information Technology (IIIT-Allahabad)
Email : javed@iiita.ac.in

Video Lectures for the book contents are available at

https://www.youtube.com/channel/UCjuoLDHnvDBenbBdFD3pQUw

Content Reference Book :
Introduction to Linear Algebra by Gilbert Strang, MIT

Dr. Mohammed Javed
Assistant Professor, Department of IT
Indian Institute of Information Technology (IIIT-Allahabad)
Email: javed@iiita.ac.in

Linear Transformations and its Applications

Change of Basis Matrix

❖ When input and output bases are same we get A as Identity Matrix
❖ When input and output bases change, we get change of basis matrix which is M

$$[M]\begin{bmatrix}1\\0\end{bmatrix}=\begin{bmatrix}3\\7\end{bmatrix} \qquad [M]\begin{bmatrix}0\\1\end{bmatrix}=\begin{bmatrix}2\\5\end{bmatrix} \qquad M=\begin{bmatrix}3&2\\7&5\end{bmatrix}$$

Wavelet Transform = Change of Wavelet Basis

❖ Wavelets are little waves
❖ They have different lengths and they are localized at different places
❖ The first basis vector is not actually a wavelet, it is the very useful flat vector of all ones
❖ Haar Wavelets Example

Dr. Mohammed Javed
Assistant Professor, Department of IT
Indian Institute of Information Technology (IIIT-Allahabad)
Email: javed@iiita.ac.in

Linear Transformations and its Applications

Haar Basis

$$w_1=\begin{bmatrix}1\\1\\1\\1\end{bmatrix} \qquad w_2=\begin{bmatrix}1\\1\\-1\\-1\end{bmatrix} \qquad w_3=\begin{bmatrix}1\\-1\\0\\0\end{bmatrix} \qquad w_4=\begin{bmatrix}0\\0\\1\\-1\end{bmatrix}$$

❖ Those vectors are orthogonal
❖ w_3 is localized in the first half and w_4 is localized in the second half
❖ The wavelet transform finds the coefficients c_1, c_2, c_3, c_4 when the input signal $v=(v_1, v_2, v_3, v_4)$
❖ The coefficients c_3 and c_4 tell us about details in the first half and last half of v
❖ The coefficient c_1 is the average

Transformation $v\ to\ c\ \rightarrow\ v=c_1w_1+c_2w_2+c_3w_3+c_4w_4=Wc$

❖ Better choice of basis of w's, 5% of the basis vector can combine to come very close to the original signal
❖ One good basis vector is flat **(1, 1, 1, 1)** retains constant background of image/signal
❖ A short wave like **(0,0,1,-1)** or in higher dimensions **(0,0,0,0,0,0,1,-1)** represents details at the end of signal

Dr. Mohammed Javed
Assistant Professor, Department of IT
Indian Institute of Information Technology (IIIT-Allahabad)
Email : javed@iiita.ac.in

Linear Transformations and its Applications

Haar Basis

❖ The Four Significant steps are:

$$\boxed{\text{Transform}} \rightarrow \boxed{\text{Compression}} \rightarrow \boxed{\text{Inverse Transform}} \rightarrow \boxed{\text{Decompression}}$$

Lossy / Lossless

❖ The transform $c = W^{-1}v$ and the reconstruction brings back $v = Wc$

$$v = \begin{bmatrix} 6 \\ 4 \\ 5 \\ 1 \end{bmatrix} \quad c = \begin{bmatrix} 4 \\ 1 \\ 1 \\ 2 \end{bmatrix} \quad \textit{The reconstruction} \quad 4w1 + w2 + w3 + w4 \quad is \quad v = Wc$$

$$= 4\begin{bmatrix} 1 \\ 1 \\ 1 \\ 1 \end{bmatrix} + \begin{bmatrix} 1 \\ 1 \\ -1 \\ -1 \end{bmatrix} + \begin{bmatrix} 1 \\ -1 \\ 0 \\ 0 \end{bmatrix} + 2\begin{bmatrix} 0 \\ 0 \\ 1 \\ -1 \end{bmatrix} = \begin{bmatrix} 1 & 1 & 1 & 0 \\ 1 & 1 & -1 & 0 \\ 1 & -1 & 0 & 1 \\ 1 & -1 & 0 & -1 \end{bmatrix}\begin{bmatrix} 4 \\ 1 \\ 1 \\ 2 \end{bmatrix} = \begin{bmatrix} 6 \\ 4 \\ 5 \\ 1 \end{bmatrix}$$

Dr. Mohammed Javed
Assistant Professor, Department of IT
Indian Institute of Information Technology (IIIT-Allahabad)
Email : javed@iiita.ac.in

Linear Transformations and its Applications

Haar Basis

❖ Those coefficients c are $W^{-1}v$

❖ Inverting this basis matrix W is easy because w's in its columns are orthogonal

❖ But they are not unit vectors, so rescale

$$v = \begin{bmatrix} 6 \\ 4 \\ 5 \\ 1 \end{bmatrix} \quad c = \begin{bmatrix} 4 \\ 1 \\ 1 \\ 2 \end{bmatrix}$$

$$W^{-1} = \begin{bmatrix} 1/4 \\ & 1/4 \\ & & 1/2 \\ & & & 1/2 \end{bmatrix}\begin{bmatrix} 1 & 1 & 1 & 1 \\ 1 & 1 & -1 & -1 \\ 1 & -1 & 0 & 0 \\ 0 & 0 & 1 & -1 \end{bmatrix}$$

$$= W^{-1}v = W^{-1}\begin{bmatrix} 6 \\ 4 \\ 5 \\ 1 \end{bmatrix} = \begin{bmatrix} 4 \\ 1 \\ 1 \\ 2 \end{bmatrix}$$

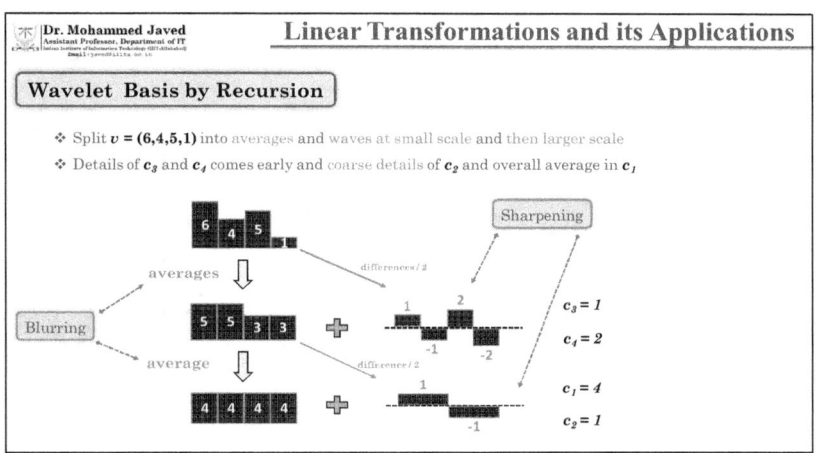

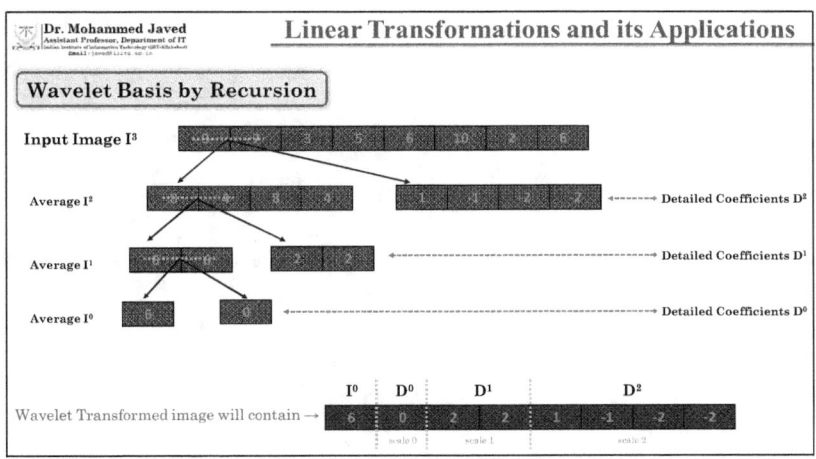

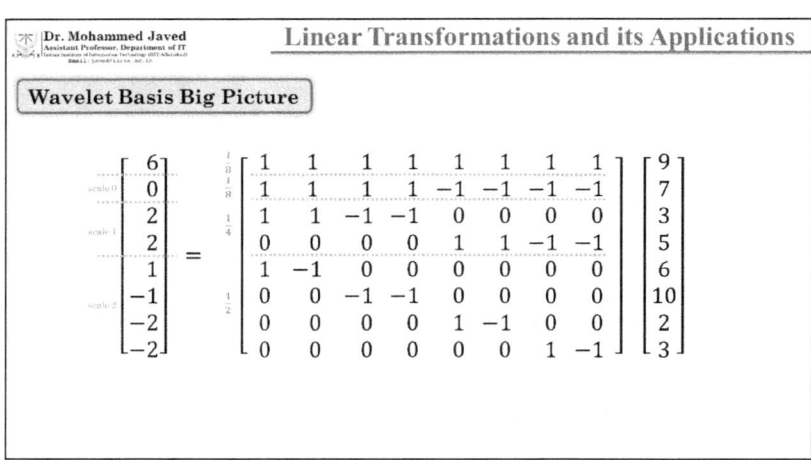

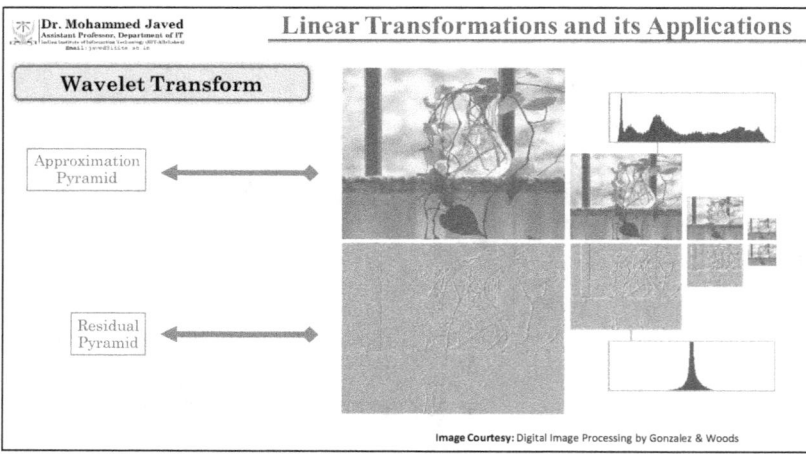

Image Courtesy: Digital Image Processing by Gonzalez & Woods

Dr. Mohammed Javed
Assistant Professor, Department of IT
Indian Institute of Information Technology (IIIT-Allahabad)
Email: javed@iiita.ac.in

Linear Transformations and its Applications

Fourier Transform (DFT) = Change of Fourier Basis

❖ The DFT involves complex numbers (powers of $e^{2\pi i/n}$)

❖ But if we choose $n = 4$, the matrices are small and the only complex number are i and $i^3 = -i$

Fourier Basis w_1 to w_n in the columns of F

$$F = \begin{bmatrix} 1 & 1 & 1 & 1 \\ 1 & i & i^2 & i^3 \\ 1 & i^2 & i^4 & i^6 \\ 1 & i^3 & i^6 & i^9 \end{bmatrix}$$

❖ The first column is the useful basis vector (1,1,1,1)

❖ It represents the average signal or the direct current (DC)

❖ It is a wave at zero frequency

❖ The third column is (1,-1,1,-1) which alternates at the highest frequency

❖ The Fourier transform decomposes the signal into waves at equally spaced frequencies.

Dr. Mohammed Javed
Assistant Professor, Department of IT
Indian Institute of Information Technology (IIIT-Allahabad)
Email: javed@iiita.ac.in

Linear Transformations and its Applications

Fourier Transform (DFT) = Change of Fourier Basis

❖ The Fourier matrix F is absolutely most important complex matrix in mathematics, Science and Engg.

❖ Fast Fourier Transform (FFT) factorizes F into matrices with many zeros

❖ The FFT has revolutionized entire Industries by speeding up of the Fourier Transform.

❖ The beautiful thing is that F^{-1} looks like F with i changes to $-i$

❖ Fourier Transform v to c, $v = c_1 w_1 + \ldots + c_n w_n = Fc$

❖ Fourier coefficients $c = F^{-1} v$

$$F^{-1} = \frac{1}{4} \begin{bmatrix} 1 & 1 & 1 & 1 \\ 1 & (-i) & (-i)^2 & (-i)^3 \\ 1 & (-i)^2 & (-i)^4 & (-i)^6 \\ 1 & (-i)^3 & (-i)^6 & (-i)^9 \end{bmatrix} = \frac{1}{4} \overline{F}$$

Discrete Cosine Transform and JPEG

Dr. Mohammed Javed
Assistant Professor, Department of IT
Indian Institute of Information Technology (IIIT-Allahabad)
Email: javed@iiita.ac.in

Video Lectures for the book contents are available at

https://www.youtube.com/channel/UCjuoLDHnvDBenbBdFD3pQUw

Content Reference Book :
Introduction to Linear Algebra by Gilbert Strang, MIT

Dr. Mohammed Javed
Assistant Professor, Department of IT

Linear Transformations and its Applications

Discrete Cosine Transform (DCT) Basis functions

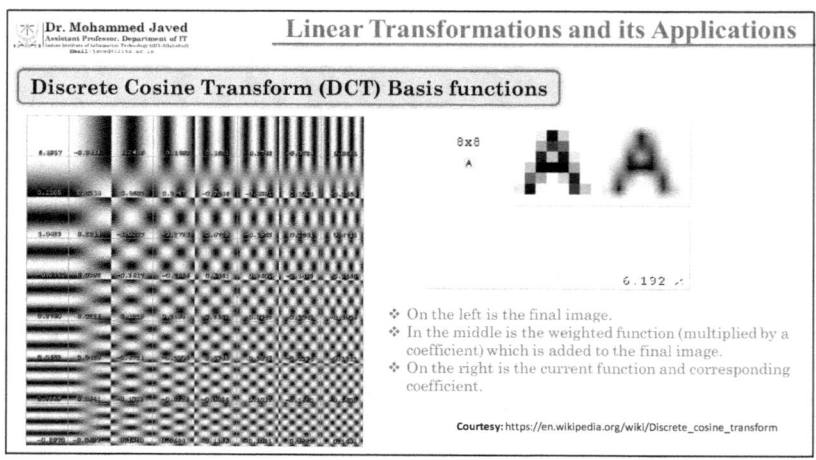

❖ On the left is the final image.
❖ In the middle is the weighted function (multiplied by a coefficient) which is added to the final image.
❖ On the right is the current function and corresponding coefficient.

Courtesy: https://en.wikipedia.org/wiki/Discrete_cosine_transform

Dr. Mohammed Javed
Assistant Professor, Department of IT
Indian Institute of Information Technology (IIIT-Allahabad)
Email: javed@iiita.ac.in

Linear Transformations and its Applications

Discrete Cosine Transform (DCT) Basis functions

❖ Distinction between a **DCT** and a **DFT** is that the **DCT** uses only cosine functions (real values)

❖ While **DFT** uses both cosines and sines (in the form of complex exponentials)

❖ Some 4×4 DCT basis matrices are shown below

❖ The basis functions are oscillating cosine waves

❖ They can also be visualized in the waveform instead of numbers

$$D_{00} = \frac{1}{4}\begin{bmatrix} 1 & 1 & 1 & 1 \\ 1 & 1 & 1 & 1 \\ 1 & 1 & 1 & 1 \\ 1 & 1 & 1 & 1 \end{bmatrix} \quad D_{02} = \frac{1}{4}\begin{bmatrix} 1 & -1 & -1 & 1 \\ 1 & -1 & -1 & 1 \\ 1 & -1 & -1 & 1 \\ 1 & -1 & -1 & 1 \end{bmatrix} \quad D_{20} = \frac{1}{4}\begin{bmatrix} 1 & 1 & 1 & 1 \\ -1 & -1 & -1 & -1 \\ -1 & -1 & -1 & -1 \\ 1 & 1 & 1 & 1 \end{bmatrix} \quad D_{22} = \frac{1}{4}\begin{bmatrix} 1 & -1 & -1 & 1 \\ -1 & 1 & 1 & -1 \\ -1 & 1 & 1 & -1 \\ 1 & -1 & -1 & 1 \end{bmatrix}$$

Dr. Mohammed Javed
Assistant Professor, Department of IT
Indian Institute of Information Technology (IIIT-Allahabad)
Email: javed@iiita.ac.in

Linear Transformations and its Applications

Discrete Cosine Transform (DCT) coefficient Computation

Pixel image of size 4×4 $P = \begin{bmatrix} 1 & 2 & 2 & -1 \\ 0 & 1 & 3 & 2 \\ 0 & 1 & 2 & 2 \\ 1 & 2 & 2 & -1 \end{bmatrix}$

Coefficient $F_{00} = D_{00} \times P = \frac{1}{4}\begin{bmatrix} 1 & 1 & 1 & 1 \\ 1 & 1 & 1 & 1 \\ 1 & 1 & 1 & 1 \\ 1 & 1 & 1 & 1 \end{bmatrix}\begin{bmatrix} 1 & 2 & 2 & -1 \\ 0 & 1 & 3 & 2 \\ 0 & 1 & 2 & 2 \\ 1 & 2 & 2 & -1 \end{bmatrix}$ $= 1 + 2 + 2 - 1 + 0 + 1 + 3 + 2 + 0 + 1 + 2 + 2 + 1 + 2 + 2 - 1 = \frac{19}{4} = 4.75$

Coefficient $F_{02} = D_{02} \times P = \frac{1}{4}\begin{bmatrix} 1 & -1 & -1 & 1 \\ 1 & -1 & -1 & 1 \\ 1 & -1 & -1 & 1 \\ 1 & -1 & -1 & 1 \end{bmatrix}\begin{bmatrix} 1 & 2 & 2 & -1 \\ 0 & 1 & 3 & 2 \\ 0 & 1 & 2 & 2 \\ 1 & 2 & 2 & -1 \end{bmatrix}$ $= 1 - 2 - 2 - 1 + 0 - 1 - 3 + 2 + 0 - 1 - 2 + 2 + 1 - 2 - 2 - 1 = \frac{-11}{4} = -2.75$

Coefficient $F_{02} = D_{22} \times P = \frac{1}{4}\begin{bmatrix} 1 & -1 & -1 & 1 \\ -1 & 1 & 1 & -1 \\ -1 & 1 & 1 & -1 \\ 1 & -1 & -1 & 1 \end{bmatrix}\begin{bmatrix} 1 & 2 & 2 & -1 \\ 0 & 1 & 3 & 2 \\ 0 & 1 & 2 & 2 \\ 1 & 2 & 2 & -1 \end{bmatrix}$ $= 1 - 2 - 2 - 1 + 0 + 1 + 3 - 2 + 0 + 1 - 2 + 2 + 1 - 2 - 2 - 1 = \frac{-5}{4} = -1.25$

$$\begin{bmatrix} 4.75 & -0.41 & -2.75 & 0.98 \\ 0.14 & -0.07 & 0.14 & 0.18 \\ -0.75 & 3.02 & -1.25 & 0.10 \\ -0.33 & 0.18 & 0.33 & 0.43 \end{bmatrix}$$

$dct2(P,4,4)$

Coefficient $F_{ij} = \begin{bmatrix} 4.75 & & -2.75 & \\ & & & \\ & & -1.25 & \\ & & & \end{bmatrix}$

Dr. Mohammed Javed
Assistant Professor, Department of IT

Linear Transformations and its Applications

Discrete Cosine Transform (DCT) coefficient Computation

❖ IDCT is used to get back the pixels back from the coefficient image

❖ We have used MATLAB command idct2 to carry out inverse transform

$$\begin{bmatrix} 4.75 & -0.41 & -2.75 & 0.98 \\ 0.14 & -0.07 & 0.14 & 0.18 \\ -0.75 & 3.02 & -1.25 & 0.10 \\ -0.33 & 0.18 & 0.33 & 0.43 \end{bmatrix} \xrightarrow{idct2(P,4,4)} \begin{bmatrix} 1 & 2 & 2 & -1 \\ 0 & 1 & 3 & 2 \\ 0 & 1 & 2 & 2 \\ 1 & 2 & 2 & -1 \end{bmatrix}$$

Dr. Mohammed Javed
Assistant Professor, Department of IT

Linear Transformations and its Applications

JPEG Compression

❖ Whole Image is divided into **8×8** Non overlapping blocks, and apply the **DCT** operation on each block.

❖ Then quantization is applied on each **DCT** block, here we get the major loss of data.

❖ We further compress all these blocks using Entropy Encoding, This is the final JPEG compressed data.

❖ Decompression process is just exactly reverse of the above whole process in reverse order.

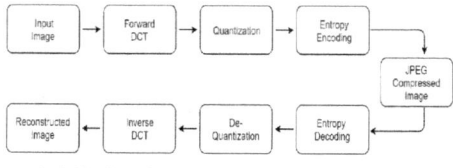

A typical flow diagram of JPEG compression and decompression processes

EigenValues and EigenVectors

 Dr. Mohammed Javed
Assistant Professor, Department of IT
Indian Institute of Information Technology (IIIT-Allahabad)
Email: javed@iiita.ac.in

Video Lectures for the book contents are available at

https://www.youtube.com/channel/UCjuoLDHnvDBenbBdFD3pQUw

Content Reference Book :
Introduction to Linear Algebra by Gilbert Strang, MIT

 Dr. Mohammed Javed
Assistant Professor, Department of IT
                                        Eigenvalues and Eigenvectors

Background

- ❖ Linear Equations $Ax = b$ come from steady state problem
- ❖ Eigen values have their greatest importance in dynamic problems
- ❖ The solution of $\frac{du}{dt} = Au$ is changing by time - growing, decaying or oscillating
- ❖ We find them by elimination method
- ❖ Another good model comes from powers of a matrix - A, A^2, A^3, ...
- ❖ Suppose you need to find the A^{100}
- ❖ The answer can be found out not by multiplying the matrix 100 times
- ❖ But with the help of Eigen values

Clock Tower @ IIIT Allahabad

Eigen values are a new way to see into the Heart of the Matrix

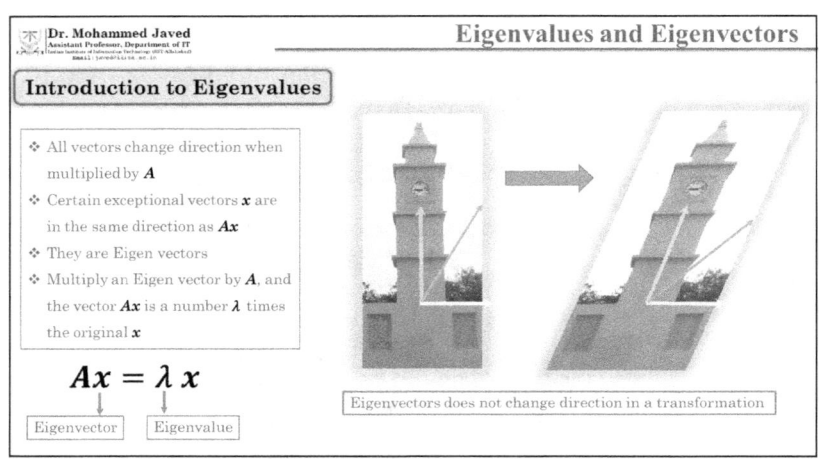

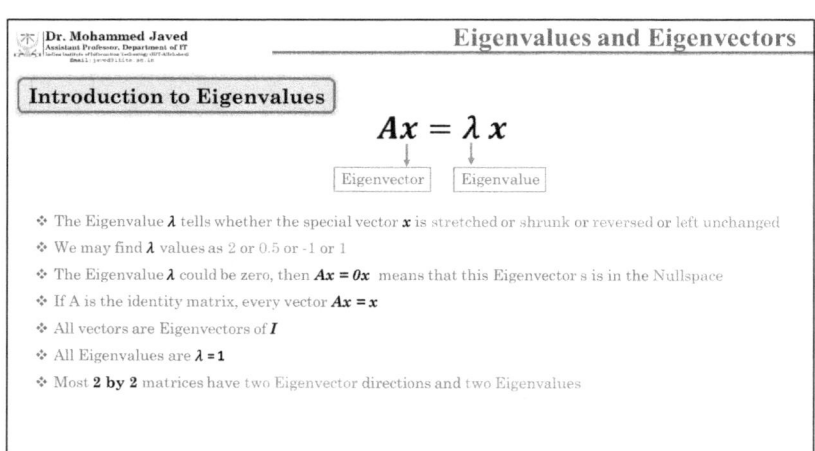

Dr. Mohammed Javed
Assistant Professor, Department of IT
Indian Institute of Information Technology (IIIT-Allahabad)
Email: javed@iiita.ac.in

Eigenvalues and Eigenvectors

Introduction to Eigenvalues

❖ The matrix A has two Eigenvalues $\lambda = 1$ and $\lambda = \frac{1}{2}$

❖ Let us see the $det(A - \lambda I) = 0$

$$A = \begin{bmatrix} 0.8 & 0.3 \\ 0.2 & 0.7 \end{bmatrix} \quad det\begin{bmatrix} 0.8 - \lambda & 0.3 \\ 0.2 & 0.7 - \lambda \end{bmatrix} = \lambda - \frac{3}{2}\lambda + \frac{1}{2} = (\lambda - 1)(\lambda - \frac{1}{2})$$

$\boxed{\lambda = 1}$ $\boxed{\lambda = \frac{1}{2}}$

❖ The Eigenvectors x_1 and x_2 are in the Nullspace of $A - I$ and $A - \frac{1}{2}I$

$(A - I)x_1 = 0 \quad Ax_1 = x_1$ the first Eigenvector is $x_1 = \begin{bmatrix} 0.6 \\ 0.4 \end{bmatrix}$

$\left(A - \frac{1}{2}I\right)x_1 = 0 \quad Ax_2 = \frac{1}{2}x_1$ the second Eigenvector is $x_2 = \begin{bmatrix} 1 \\ -1 \end{bmatrix}$

$$Ax_1 = \begin{bmatrix} 0.8 & 0.3 \\ 0.2 & 0.7 \end{bmatrix}\begin{bmatrix} 0.6 \\ 0.4 \end{bmatrix} = x_1 \qquad Ax_2 = \begin{bmatrix} 0.8 & 0.3 \\ 0.2 & 0.7 \end{bmatrix}\begin{bmatrix} 1 \\ -1 \end{bmatrix} = x_2$$

Dr. Mohammed Javed
Assistant Professor, Department of IT
Indian Institute of Information Technology (IIIT-Allahabad)
Email: javed@iiita.ac.in

Eigenvalues and Eigenvectors

Introduction to Eigenvalues

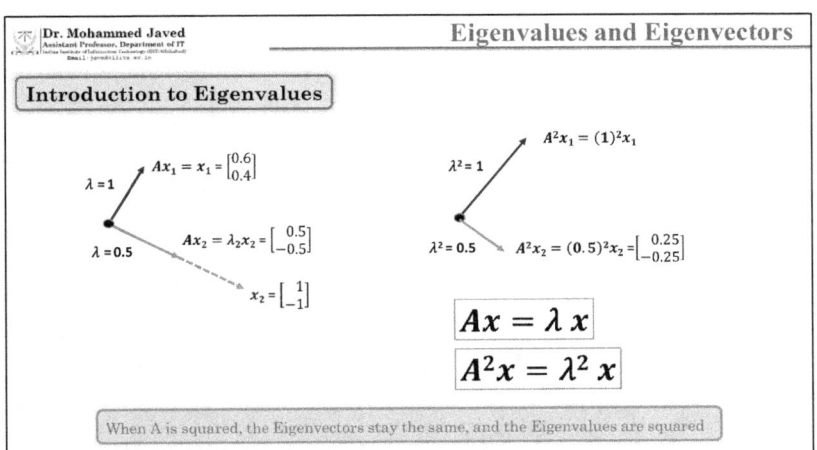

$\lambda = 1$ $Ax_1 = x_1 = \begin{bmatrix} 0.6 \\ 0.4 \end{bmatrix}$

$\lambda = 0.5$ $Ax_2 = \lambda_2 x_2 = \begin{bmatrix} 0.5 \\ -0.5 \end{bmatrix}$

$x_2 = \begin{bmatrix} 1 \\ -1 \end{bmatrix}$

$\lambda^2 = 1$ $A^2x_1 = (1)^2 x_1$

$\lambda^2 = 0.5$ $A^2x_2 = (0.5)^2 x_2 = \begin{bmatrix} 0.25 \\ -0.25 \end{bmatrix}$

$$\boxed{Ax = \lambda x}$$
$$\boxed{A^2x = \lambda^2 x}$$

When A is squared, the Eigenvectors stay the same, and the Eigenvalues are squared

---

Linear Algebra Concepts with Real Life
Applications

Dr. Mohammed Javed
Assistant Professor, Department of IT

Eigenvalues and Eigenvectors

Introduction to Eigenvalues

$A = \begin{bmatrix} 0.8 & 0.3 \\ 0.2 & 0.7 \end{bmatrix}$ $\lambda_1 = 1$ $\lambda_2 = \frac{1}{2}$ $x_1 = \begin{bmatrix} 0.6 \\ 0.4 \end{bmatrix}$ $x_2 = \begin{bmatrix} 1 \\ -1 \end{bmatrix}$

❖ The example for A^{100}

❖ The Eigenvectors of are same as x_1 and x_2

❖ The Eigenvalues of A^{100} are $1^{100} = 1$ and $\left(\frac{1}{2}\right)^{100}$ = very small number

❖ Each Eigenvector is multiplied by its Eigenvalue, when we multiply by A

❖ We didn't need these Eigenvectors to find A^2

❖ At every step x_1 is unchanged and x_2 is multiplied by $\left(\frac{1}{2}\right)$, so we have $\left(\frac{1}{2}\right)^{99}$

$$A^{99} \begin{bmatrix} 0.8 \\ 0.2 \end{bmatrix} \text{ is really } x1 + (0.2)\left(\frac{1}{2}\right)^{99} x_2 = \begin{bmatrix} 0.6 \\ 0.4 \end{bmatrix} + \begin{bmatrix} very \\ Small \\ vetor \end{bmatrix}$$

❖ This is the first column of A^{100}

A is a *Markov Matrix*

❖ The Eigenvector x_1 is a steady state that does not change ($\lambda_1 = 1$)

❖ The Eigenvector x_2 is a decaying mode that virtually disappears ($\lambda_2 = 0.5$)

❖ Higher the power of A, the closer its columns approach the steady state

---

Dr. Mohammed Javed
Assistant Professor, Department of IT

Eigenvalues and Eigenvectors

Introduction to Eigenvalues

❖ Given a **2 by 2** matrix A with two Eigenvalues λ_1 and λ_2

$$A = \begin{bmatrix} a & c \\ b & d \end{bmatrix}$$

❖ Sum of Eigenvalues $\lambda_1 + \lambda_2$ = TRACE of the Matrix

$$\lambda_1 + \lambda_2 = a + b$$

❖ Product of Eigenvalues $\lambda_1 \times \lambda_2$ = DETERMINANT of the Matrix

$$\lambda_1 \times \lambda_2 = ad - bc$$

$A = \begin{bmatrix} 0.8 & 0.3 \\ 0.2 & 0.7 \end{bmatrix}$ $\lambda_1 = 1$ $\lambda_2 = \frac{1}{2}$

Dr. Mohammed Javed
Assistant Professor, Department of IT
Indian Institute of Information Technology (IIIT-Allahabad)
Email: javed@iiita.ac.in

Eigenvalues and Eigenvectors

Introduction to Eigenvalues

❖ The Projection Matrix $P = \begin{bmatrix} 0.5 & 0.5 \\ 0.5 & 0.5 \end{bmatrix}$ has Eigenvalues $\lambda_1 = 1$ and $\lambda_2 = 0$

❖ Its Eigenvectors are $x_1 = \begin{bmatrix} 1 \\ 1 \end{bmatrix}$ and $x_2 = \begin{bmatrix} 1 \\ -1 \end{bmatrix}$

❖ For those vector $Px_1 = x_1$ (steady state) and $Px_2 = 0$ (Nullspace)

❖ This example illustrates Markov matrices and singular matrices, and symmetric matrices

❖ All have special λ 's and x 's

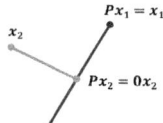

   1. Each column of $P = \begin{bmatrix} 0.5 & 0.5 \\ 0.5 & 0.5 \end{bmatrix}$ adds to 1, so $\lambda = 1$ is an Eigenvalue

   2. P is singular, so $\lambda = 0$ is an Eigenvalue

   3. P is symmetric, so its Eigenvectors $\begin{bmatrix} 1 \\ 1 \end{bmatrix}$ and $\begin{bmatrix} 1 \\ -1 \end{bmatrix}$ are perpendicular

   Projection keeps the column space and destroys the Nullspace

---

Dr. Mohammed Javed
Assistant Professor, Department of IT
Indian Institute of Information Technology (IIIT-Allahabad)
Email: javed@iiita.ac.in

Eigenvalues and Eigenvectors

Introduction to Eigenvalues

❖ The Reflection Matrix $R = \begin{bmatrix} 0 & 1 \\ 1 & 0 \end{bmatrix}$ has Eigenvalues $\lambda_1 = 1$ and $\lambda_2 = -1$

❖ The Eigenvector $x_1 = \begin{bmatrix} 1 \\ 1 \end{bmatrix}$ is unchanged by R

❖ The second Eigenvector is $x_2 = \begin{bmatrix} 1 \\ -1 \end{bmatrix}$ its signs are reversed by R

❖ The Eigenvectors for R are the same as for P, because *Reflection = 2 Projection - I*

$$R = 2P - I \quad = \begin{bmatrix} 0 & 1 \\ 1 & 0 \end{bmatrix} = 2\begin{bmatrix} 0.5 & 0.5 \\ 0.5 & 0.5 \end{bmatrix} - \begin{bmatrix} 1 & 0 \\ 0 & 1 \end{bmatrix}$$

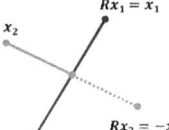

❖ If $Px = \lambda x$, then $2Px = 2\lambda x$

❖ The Eigenvalues are doubled when the matrix is doubled

❖ Now subtract $Ix = x$, result is $(2P - I)x = (2\lambda - 1)x$

❖ When a matrix is shifted by I, each λ is shifted by 1

❖ No change in Eigenvectors

Dr. Mohammed Javed
Assistant Professor, Department of IT
Indian Institute of Information Technology (IIIT-Allahabad)
Email : javed@iiita.ac.in
Eigenvalues and Eigenvectors

Introduction to Eigenvalues

❖ If $A = \begin{bmatrix} 1 & 2 \\ 2 & 4 \end{bmatrix}$ is already singular (Zero determinant). Find its λ's and x's

❖ When A is singular, then $\lambda = 0$ is one of the Eigenvalues

Subtract λ from the diagonal to find $A - \lambda I = \begin{bmatrix} 1-\lambda & 2 \\ 2 & 4-\lambda \end{bmatrix}$

Take determinant $det \begin{bmatrix} 1-\lambda & 2 \\ 2 & 4-\lambda \end{bmatrix} = (1-\lambda)(4-\lambda) - (2)(2) = \lambda^2 - 5\lambda$

Set the determinant $\lambda^2 - 5\lambda = 0$ $\boxed{\lambda_1 = 0 \text{ and } \lambda_2 = 5}$

Now find Eigenvectors   *Solve $(A - \lambda I)x = 0$ separtely for $\lambda_1 = 0$* and $\lambda_2 = 5$

$(A - 0\,I)x = \begin{bmatrix} 1 & 2 \\ 2 & 4 \end{bmatrix}\begin{bmatrix} y \\ z \end{bmatrix} = \begin{bmatrix} 0 \\ 0 \end{bmatrix}$ *yields an Eigenvector* $x_1 = \begin{bmatrix} y \\ z \end{bmatrix} = \begin{bmatrix} 2 \\ -1 \end{bmatrix}$ *for $\lambda_1 = 0$*

$(A - 5\,I)x = \begin{bmatrix} -4 & 2 \\ 2 & -1 \end{bmatrix}\begin{bmatrix} y \\ z \end{bmatrix} = \begin{bmatrix} 0 \\ 0 \end{bmatrix}$ *yields an Eigenvector* $x_1 = \begin{bmatrix} y \\ z \end{bmatrix} = \begin{bmatrix} 1 \\ 2 \end{bmatrix}$ *for $\lambda_2 = 5$*

Dr. Mohammed Javed
Assistant Professor, Department of IT
Indian Institute of Information Technology (IIIT-Allahabad)
Email : javed@iiita.ac.in
Eigenvalues and Eigenvectors

Introduction to Eigenvalues

❖ Steps for solving the Eigenvalue problem for an *n by n* matrix, follow these steps

1. Compute the determinant of $A - \lambda I$ with subtracted along the diagonal.

2. Find the roots of this polynomial, by solving $\det(A - \lambda I) = 0$

3. For each Eigenvalue λ, Solve $(A - \lambda I)x = 0$ to find an Eigenvector x

---

Dr. Mohammed Javed
Assistant Professor, Department of IT
Indian Institute of Information Technology (IIIT-Allahabad)
Email: javed@iiita.ac.in

Eigenvalues and Eigenvectors

Introduction to Eigenvalues

❖ Imaginary Eigenvalues

❖ The 90° rotation $Q = \begin{bmatrix} 0 & -1 \\ 1 & 0 \end{bmatrix}$ has no real Eigenvectors

❖ Its Eigenvalues are $\lambda = i$ and $\lambda = -i$

❖ Sum of $\lambda's$ = Trace = 0

❖ Product of $\lambda's$ = Determinant = 1

❖ After a rotation, no vector Qx stays in the same direction as x (except $x = 0$)

❖ There cannot be an Eigenvector, unless we go to imaginary numbers

$$\boxed{Q - \lambda I = 0} \qquad \boxed{\lambda^2 + 1 = 0} \qquad \boxed{\lambda = i \text{ and } \lambda = -i}$$

Complex Eigenvectors $\qquad \begin{bmatrix} 0 & -1 \\ 1 & 0 \end{bmatrix}\begin{bmatrix} 1 \\ i \end{bmatrix} = -i \begin{bmatrix} 1 \\ i \end{bmatrix} \qquad \begin{bmatrix} 0 & -1 \\ 1 & 0 \end{bmatrix}\begin{bmatrix} i \\ 1 \end{bmatrix} = i \begin{bmatrix} i \\ 1 \end{bmatrix}$

Singular Value Decomposition

Dr. Mohammed Javed
Assistant Professor, Department of IT
Indian Institute of Information Technology (IIIT-Allahabad)
Email: javed@iiita.ac.in

Video Lectures for the book contents are available at

https://www.youtube.com/channel/UCjuoLDHnvDBenbBdFD3pQUw

Content Reference Book :
Introduction to Linear Algebra by Gilbert Strang, MIT

Dr. Mohammed Javed
Assistant Professor, Department of IT
Indian Institute of Information Technology (IIIT-Allahabad)
Email: javed@iiita.ac.in

Singular Value Decomposition

Background

- ❖ SVD joins with LU from elimination and QR from Orthogonalization
- ❖ SVD stands for Singular Value Decomposition
- ❖ SVD can deals the rectangular matrices, every matrix is broken down into $A = U \Sigma V^T$
- ❖ The diagonal matrix Σ has Eigenvalues from $A^T A$ not from A
- ❖ These positive entries (called as sigma) will be $\sigma_1, \sigma_2, \ldots, \sigma_r$
- ❖ They are singular values of A
- ❖ They will fill the first r places on the main diagonal of Σ - when A has rank r
- ❖ Rest of the Σ is zero
- ❖ With rectangular matrices $A^T A$ and $A A^T$ are the key

---

Dr. Mohammed Javed
Assistant Professor, Department of IT
Indian Institute of Information Technology (IIIT-Allahabad)
Email: javed@iiita.ac.in

Singular Value Decomposition

Background

Singular Value Decomposition: Any $m \times n$ matrix can be factored into

$$A = U \Sigma V^T \quad = (Orthogonal)(diagonal)(orthogonal)$$

- ❖ The columns of U (m by m) are Eigenvectors of $A A^T$
- ❖ The columns of V (n by n) are Eigenvectors of $A^T A$
- ❖ The r singular values on the diagonal of Σ (m by n)
- ❖ They are the square roots of the non zero Eigenvalues of both $A A^T$ and $A^T A$

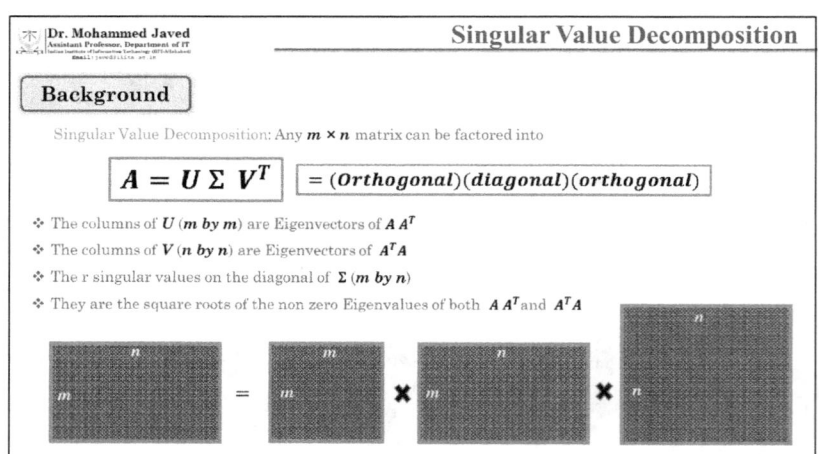

Dr. Mohammed Javed
Assistant Professor, Department of IT

Singular Value Decomposition

SVD – Geometrical Interpretation

Singular Value Decomposition: Any $m \times n$ matrix can be factored into

$$A = U \Sigma V^T \quad = (Orthogonal)(diagonal)(orthogonal)$$

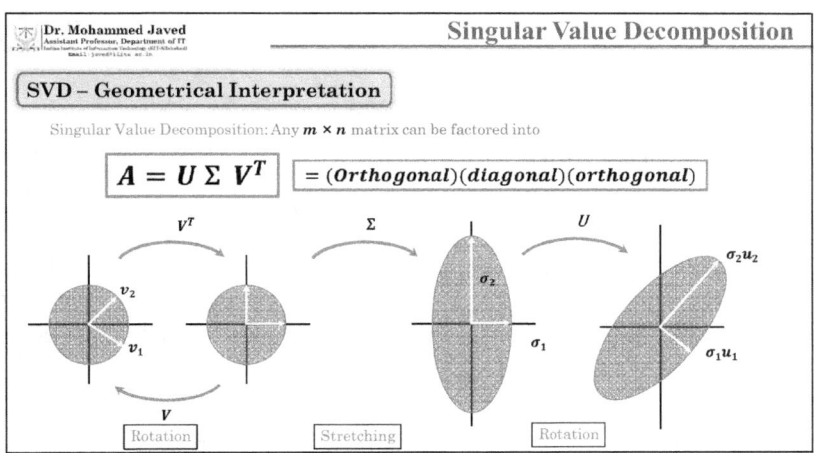

Dr. Mohammed Javed
Assistant Professor, Department of IT

Singular Value Decomposition

 **Background**

❖ For positive definite matrices, Σ is Λ and $U \Sigma V^T$ is identical of $Q \Lambda Q^T$

❖ SVD choses those bases in an extremely special way

❖ When A multiplies a column v_j of V, it produces σ_j times a column of U

❖ Eigenvectors of $A A^T$ and $A^T A$ must go into the columns of U and V

$$A A^T = (U \Sigma V^T)(V \Sigma^T U^T) = U \Sigma \Sigma^T U^T \qquad A^T A = V \Sigma^T \Sigma V^T$$

❖ U matrix must be Eigenvector matrix for $A A^T$

❖ V matrix must be Eigenvector matrix for $A^T A$

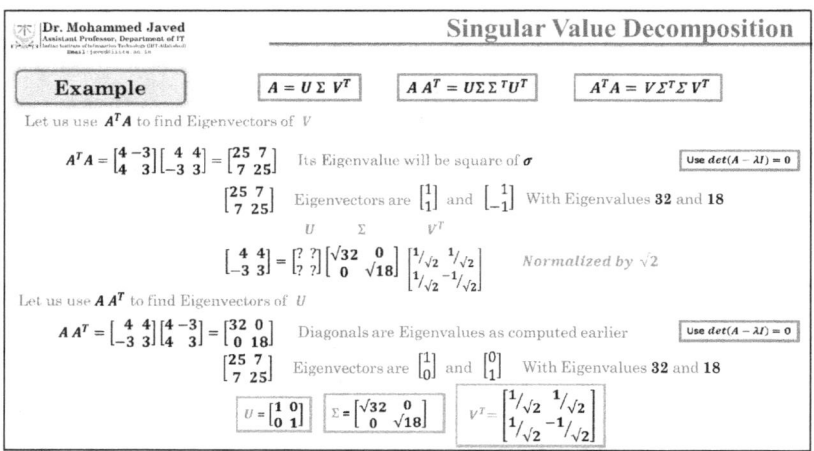

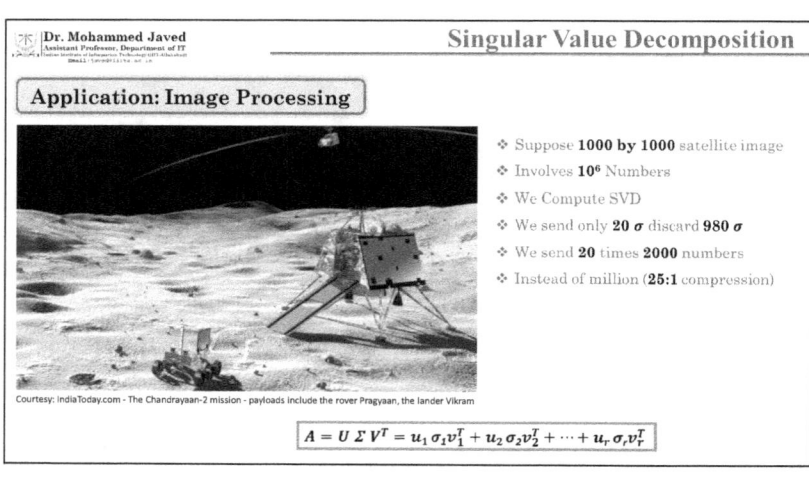

Dr. Mohammed Javed
Assistant Professor, Department of IT
Indian Institute of Information Technology (IIIT-Allahabad)
Email: javed@iiita.ac.in

Singular Value Decomposition

Application: Image and Video Processing

❖ An image is a large matrix of grayscale values, one for each pixel and colour

❖ When nearby pixels are correlated (not random) the image can be compressed

❖ Edges in image (sudden change in grayscale) are the hard parts to compress

❖ For videos, not much data changes are observed between frames

❖ The SVD separates any matrix A into rank one pieces $uv^T = (column)(row)$

❖ The columns and rows are Eigenvectors of symmetric matrices AA^T and A^TA

❖ A is often rectangular, but AA^T and A^TA are square, symmetric, and positive definite

---

Dr. Mohammed Javed
Assistant Professor, Department of IT
Indian Institute of Information Technology (IIIT-Allahabad)
Email: javed@iiita.ac.in

Singular Value Decomposition

Application: Image Processing and Compression

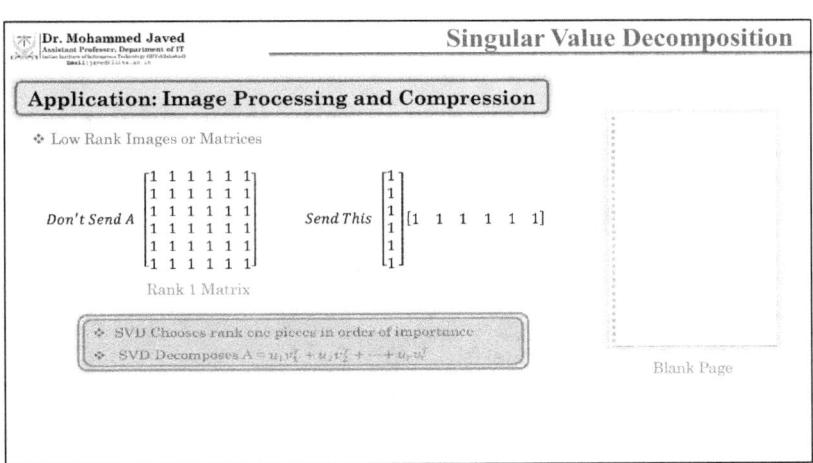

❖ Low Rank Images or Matrices

$$Don't\ Send\ A \begin{bmatrix} 1 & 1 & 1 & 1 & 1 & 1 \\ 1 & 1 & 1 & 1 & 1 & 1 \\ 1 & 1 & 1 & 1 & 1 & 1 \\ 1 & 1 & 1 & 1 & 1 & 1 \\ 1 & 1 & 1 & 1 & 1 & 1 \\ 1 & 1 & 1 & 1 & 1 & 1 \end{bmatrix} \qquad Send\ This \begin{bmatrix} 1 \\ 1 \\ 1 \\ 1 \\ 1 \\ 1 \end{bmatrix} \begin{bmatrix} 1 & 1 & 1 & 1 & 1 & 1 \end{bmatrix}$$

Rank 1 Matrix

❖ SVD Chooses rank one pieces in order of importance
❖ SVD Decomposes $A = u_1 v_1^T + u_2 v_2^T + \cdots + u_r v_r^T$

Blank Page

Dr. Mohammed Javed
Assistant Professor, Department of IT

Singular Value Decomposition

SVD- Eigenvectors in Images

❖ Eigenvectors of most images are not orthogonal

❖ Furthermore, the Eigenvectors x_1, x_2 give only one set of vectors, and we want two sets (u's and v's)

❖ The answer to these difficulties in the SVD

❖ Use Eigenvectors u of AA^T and the eigenvectors of v of A^TA

❖ Since AA^T and A^TA are symmetric, the u's will be one orthogonal set and v's will be another orthogonal set

❖ Then rank 2 matrix will be $A = \sigma_1 u_1 v_1^T + \sigma_2 u_2 v_2^T$

❖ The size of σ_1 and σ_2 will decide whether they can be ignored while compression

❖ We keep larger σ's and ignore small σ's

❖ Images mostly have full rank

❖ But they do have low effective rank

❖ Means: many singular values are small and can be set to zero

❖ We transmit a low rank approximation

Dr. Mohammed Javed
Assistant Professor, Department of IT

Singular Value Decomposition

Flags with Finite Rank

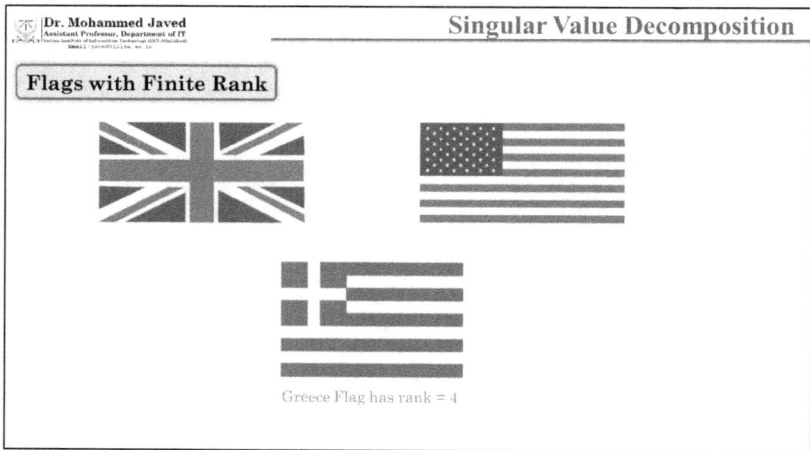

Greece Flag has rank = 4

Orthogonality

Dr. Mohammed Javed
Assistant Professor, Department of IT
Indian Institute of Information Technology (IIIT-Allahabad)
Email:javed@iiita.ac.in

Video Lectures for the book contents are available at

https://www.youtube.com/channel/UCjuoLDHnvDBenbBdFD3pQUw

Content Reference Book :
Introduction to Linear Algebra by Gilbert Strang, MIT

Dr. Mohammed Javed
Assistant Professor, Department of IT
Indian Institute of Information Technology (IIIT-Allahabad)
Email: javed@iiita.ac.in

Orthogonal Vectors and Subspaces

Foundation

❖ If A is a rectangular matrix, $Ax = b$ is often unsolvable
❖ The matrix A^TA will help us find a vector $\hat{x}$
❖ That comes as close as possible to solving $Ax = b$

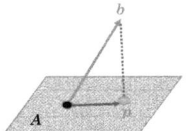

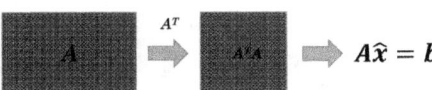

$$A\hat{x} = b$$

❖ Foundation for Projections on subspaces
❖ Approximations

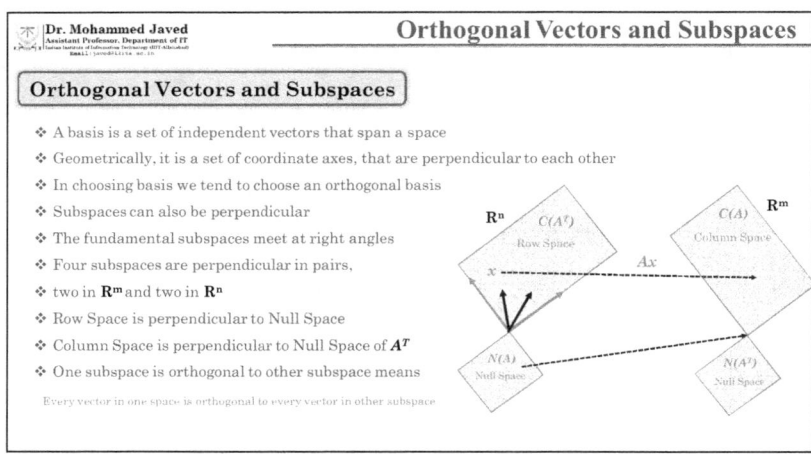

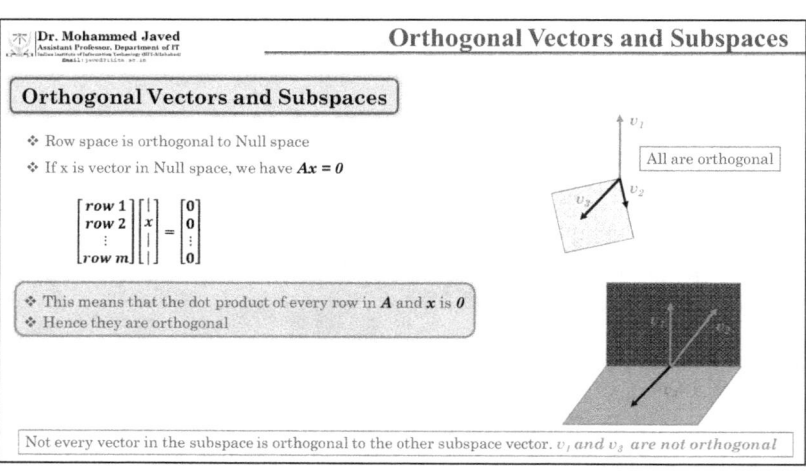

Dr. Mohammed Javed
Assistant Professor, Department of IT
Indian Institute of Information Technology (IIIT-Allahabad)
Email : javed@iiita.ac.in

Orthogonal Vectors and Subspaces

Orthogonal Vectors and Subspaces

❖ Orthogonal is the another word for Perpendicular or forming a Right angled triangle

❖ Length of a vector or Norm is denoted as $\|x\|$

❖ In two dimensions it comes from the hypotenuse of a right triangle

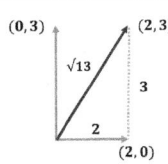

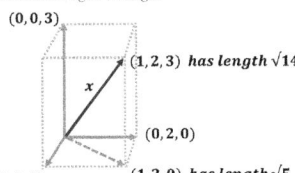

$(1,2,3)$ *has length* $\sqrt{14}$

$(1,2,0)$ *has length* $\sqrt{5}$

Length in 2D $\|x\|^2 = x_1^2 + x_2^2 = \sqrt{x_1^2 + x_2^2}$	Length in 3D $\|x\|^2 = x_1^2 + x_2^2 + x_3^2 = \sqrt{x_1^2 + x_2^2 + x_3^2}$

Dr. Mohammed Javed
Assistant Professor, Department of IT
Indian Institute of Information Technology (IIIT-Allahabad)
Email : javed@iiita.ac.in

Orthogonal Vectors and Subspaces

Orthogonal Vectors and Subspaces

❖ Length of the vector is also represented $x^T x$

$$x^T x = \begin{bmatrix} 1 \\ 2 \\ -3 \end{bmatrix} [1 \quad 2 \quad -3] = 1^2 + 2^2 + 3^2 = 14$$

❖ Two vectors are orthogonal if their inner product is Zero

$$x^T y = [x_1 \ \ldots \ x_n] \begin{bmatrix} y_1 \\ \vdots \\ y_n \end{bmatrix} = x_1 y_1 + \cdots + x_n y_n = 0$$

$x^T y = 0$

$x^T y > 0$

$x^T y < 0$

❖ If $x^T y > 0$, then their angle is less than $90°$

❖ If $x^T y < 0$, then their angle is greater than $90°$

❖ In $x^T y$ generally x refers to Matrix X

If non zero vectors $v_1, v_2, \ldots, v_k$ are mutually orthogonal, then those vectors are linearly independent

Orthogonal Vectors and Subspaces

Dr. Mohammed Javed
Assistant Professor, Department of IT
Indian Institute of Information Technology (IIIT-Allahabad)
Email: javed@iiita.ac.in

Orthogonal Vectors and Subspaces

❖ Show that the two vectors x and y are orthogonal

$$x = \begin{bmatrix} 1 \\ 2 \\ 3 \end{bmatrix} \qquad y = \begin{bmatrix} 2 \\ -1 \\ 0 \end{bmatrix} \qquad x^T y = \begin{bmatrix} 1 \\ 2 \\ 3 \end{bmatrix} \begin{bmatrix} 2 & -1 & 0 \end{bmatrix} = 2 - 2 + 0 = 0$$

❖ How to prove $x^T y = 0$

By Pythagoras's Theorem $\|x\|^2 + \|y\|^2 = \|x + y\|^2$

$$x^T x + y^T y = (x + y)^T (x + y)$$

$$2\, x^T y = 0$$

$$\boxed{x^T y = 0}$$

Projections

Dr. Mohammed Javed
Assistant Professor, Department of IT
Indian Institute of Information Technology (IIIT-Allahabad)
Email: javed@iiita.ac.in

Video Lectures for the book contents are available at

https://www.youtube.com/channel/UCjuoLDHnvDBenbBdFD3pQUw

Content Reference Book :
Introduction to Linear Algebra by Gilbert Strang, MIT

Dr. Mohammed Javed
Assistant Professor, Department of IT

Projections and Subspaces

Cosines and Projections onto Lines

❖ Vectors with $x^T y$ are orthogonal

❖ Now we want to know inner products that are not zero, and angles that are not right angles

❖ Suppose, we want to find the distance from a point b to the line in the direction of the vector a

❖ Projection p is the point closest to b

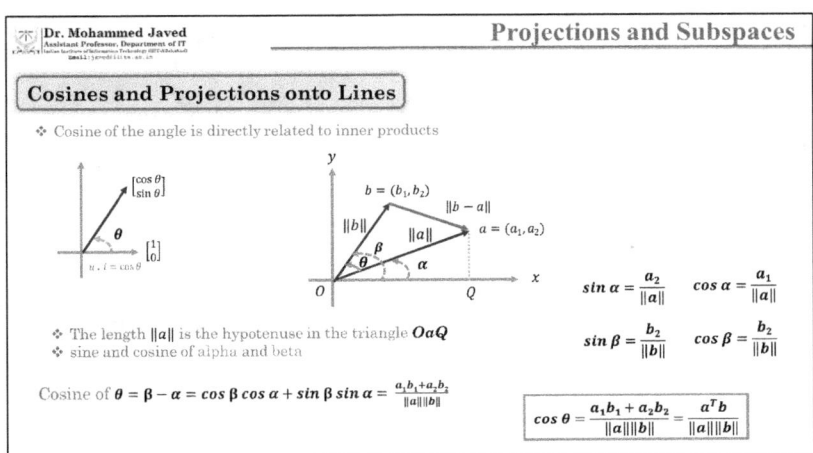

$e = b - p$

p = Projection of b onto line through a

❖ This problem leads to least square solution to an undetermined system
❖ Vector b represents the data from experiments
❖ In Economics, Statistics it is called regression analysis

Dr. Mohammed Javed
Assistant Professor, Department of IT

Projections and Subspaces

Cosines and Projections onto Lines

❖ Cosine of the angle is directly related to inner products

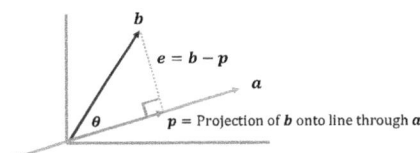

$b = (b_1, b_2)$
$a = (a_1, a_2)$

❖ The length $\|a\|$ is the hypotenuse in the triangle OaQ
❖ sine and cosine of alpha and beta

$$\sin \alpha = \frac{a_2}{\|a\|} \qquad \cos \alpha = \frac{a_1}{\|a\|}$$

$$\sin \beta = \frac{b_2}{\|b\|} \qquad \cos \beta = \frac{b_2}{\|b\|}$$

Cosine of $\theta = \beta - \alpha = \cos \beta \cos \alpha + \sin \beta \sin \alpha = \frac{a_1 b_1 + a_2 b_2}{\|a\|\|b\|}$

$$\cos \theta = \frac{a_1 b_1 + a_2 b_2}{\|a\|\|b\|} = \frac{a^T b}{\|a\|\|b\|}$$

Dr. Mohammed Javed
Assistant Professor, Department of IT
Indian Institute of Information Technology (IIIT-Allahabad)
Email : javed@iiita.ac.in

Projections and Subspaces

Projections onto Lines

❖ Projection of a point b onto a line a is p, which is some multiple $p = \hat{x}a$

❖ The line from b to the closest point $p = \hat{x}a$ is perpendicular to the vector a

$$\boxed{b - \hat{x}a \perp a} \qquad \boxed{a^T(b - \hat{x}a) = 0} \qquad \boxed{\hat{x} = \frac{a^T b}{a^T a}}$$

Now, we know $p = \hat{x}a$

$$\boxed{p = \hat{x}a = \frac{a^T b}{a^T a}a}$$

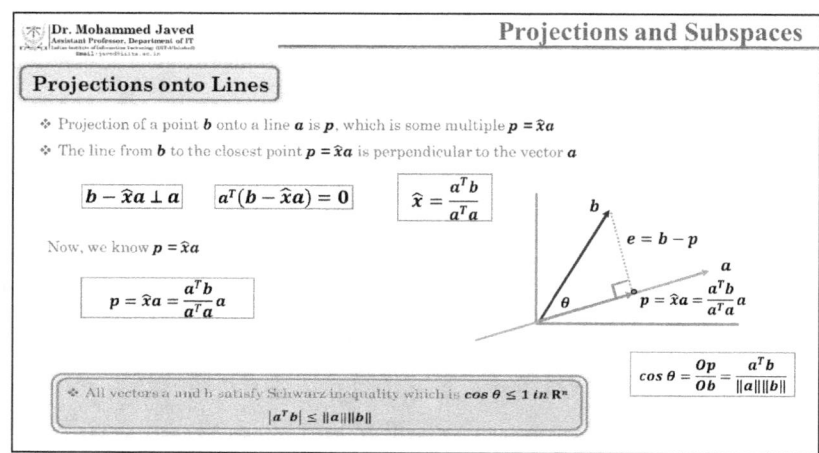

$$e = b - p$$

$$p = \hat{x}a = \frac{a^T b}{a^T a}a$$

❖ All vectors a and b satisfy Schwarz inequality which is $cos\ \theta \leq 1\ in\ \mathbb{R}^n$

$$|a^T b| \leq \|a\|\|b\|$$

$$\boxed{cos\ \theta = \frac{Op}{Ob} = \frac{a^T b}{\|a\|\|b\|}}$$

Dr. Mohammed Javed
Assistant Professor, Department of IT
Indian Institute of Information Technology (IIIT-Allahabad)
Email : javed@iiita.ac.in

Projections and Subspaces

Projections onto Lines

❖ Project $b = (1, 2, 3)$ onto a line through $a=(1, 1, 1)$ to get $\hat{x}$ and p

$$\hat{x} = \frac{a^T b}{a^T a} = \frac{6}{3} = 2$$

Projection $p = \hat{x}a = (2, 2, 2)$

The angle between a and b has

$$cos\ \theta = \frac{\|p\|}{\|b\|} = \frac{\sqrt{12}}{\sqrt{14}}$$

$$cos\ \theta = \frac{a^T b}{\|a\|\|b\|} = \frac{6}{\sqrt{3}\sqrt{14}}$$

Schwarz inequality which is $|a^T b| \leq \|a\|\|b\|$ is $6 \leq \sqrt{3}\sqrt{14}$

If we write **6** and $\sqrt{36}$, then $\sqrt{36} \leq \sqrt{42}$ Also cosine is less than 1, because b is not parallel to a

---

Dr. Mohammed Javed
Assistant Professor, Department of IT
Indian Institute of Information Technology (IIIT-Allahabad)
Email: javed@iiita.ac.in

Projections and Subspaces

Projections onto Lines

❖ Projection of b onto a line through a lies at

$$p = \hat{x}a = \frac{a^T b}{a^T a}a$$

Rewrite as

$$p = a\frac{a^T b}{a^T a}$$ Therefore the Projection Matrix $$P = \frac{a\,a^T}{a^T a}$$

$$p = Pb$$

P is a matrix that multiplies b and produces p

❖ This is column times a row — a square matrix — divided by the number $a^T a$

Dr. Mohammed Javed
Assistant Professor, Department of IT
Indian Institute of Information Technology (IIIT-Allahabad)
Email: javed@iiita.ac.in

Projections and Subspaces

Projections onto Lines

❖ The matrix that projects onto the line through $a = (1,1,1)$ is

$$P = \frac{a\,a^T}{a^T a} = \frac{1}{3}\begin{bmatrix}1\\1\\1\end{bmatrix}\begin{bmatrix}1 & 1 & 1\end{bmatrix} = \begin{bmatrix}1/3 & 1/3 & 1/3\\1/3 & 1/3 & 1/3\\1/3 & 1/3 & 1/3\end{bmatrix}$$

❖ P is symmetric matrix
❖ P remains same if a is doubled
❖ Its square is itself $P^2 = P$

$$= \frac{1}{12}\begin{bmatrix}2\\2\\2\end{bmatrix}\begin{bmatrix}2 & 2 & 2\end{bmatrix} = \begin{bmatrix}1/3 & 1/3 & 1/3\\1/3 & 1/3 & 1/3\\1/3 & 1/3 & 1/3\end{bmatrix}$$

Same as before

Dr. Mohammed Javed
Assistant Professor, Department of IT
Indian Institute of Information Technology (IIIT-Allahabad)
Email: javed@iiita.ac.in

Projections and Subspaces

Projections onto Lines

❖ Project onto the θ *direction* in the xy plane

❖ The line goes through $a = (cos\ \theta,\ sin\ \theta)$ and the matrix is symmetric with $P^2 = P$

$$P = \frac{a\,a^T}{a^T a} = \begin{bmatrix} c \\ s \end{bmatrix} [c \quad s] = \begin{bmatrix} c^2 & cs \\ cs & s^2 \end{bmatrix}$$

❖ To project b onto a, multiply by the projection matrix P: $p = Pb$

Dr. Mohammed Javed
Assistant Professor, Department of IT
Indian Institute of Information Technology (IIIT-Allahabad)
Email: javed@iiita.ac.in

Projections and Subspaces

Projections onto a Plane

❖ Now, I will tell you two basis from the plane which may not be ⊥ (a_1 and a_2), but independent

❖ We have $e = b - p$ which is ⊥ to the plane A

$p = \hat{x}_1 a_1 + \hat{x}_2 a_2$ some multiple of basis

$p = A\hat{x}$

We have projection $p = A\hat{x}$ therefore find $\hat{x}$

We have $e = b - A\hat{x}$ is ⊥ to the plane A

We get 2 Equations $a_1^T(b - A\hat{x}) = 0 \qquad a_2^T(b - A\hat{x}) = 0$

Put in matrix form $\begin{bmatrix} a_1^T \\ a_2^T \end{bmatrix}(b - A\hat{x}) = \begin{bmatrix} 0 \\ 0 \end{bmatrix}$

Therefore $A^T(b - A\hat{x}) = 0$

Rewrite as $A^T A\hat{x} = A^T b$

$\boxed{\hat{x} = (A^T A)^{-1} A^T b}$ $\boxed{\text{projection } p = A\hat{x} = A(A^T A)^{-1} A^T b}$ $\boxed{\text{Projection Matrix } P = A(A^T A)^{-1} A^T}$

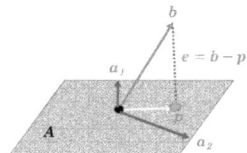

$\text{Column Space of } A = \begin{bmatrix} | & | \\ a_1 & a_2 \\ | & | \end{bmatrix}$

Least Square Fitting

Dr. Mohammed Javed
Assistant Professor, Department of IT
Indian Institute of Information Technology (IIIT-Allahabad)
Email:javed@iiita.ac.in

Video Lectures for the book contents are available at

https://www.youtube.com/channel/UCjuoLDHnvDBenbBdFD3pQUw

Content Reference Book :
Introduction to Linear Algebra by Gilbert Strang, MIT

Dr. Mohammed Javed
Assistant Professor, Department of IT
Indian Institute of Information Technology (IIIT-Allahabad)
Email: javed@iiita.ac.in

Projection Matrices and Least Squares

Least Squares Fitting of Data

❖ Suppose we do series of experiments, and expect the output b to be a linear function of the input t

❖ We look for a straight line $b = C + Dt$

❖ Suppose the observations are noted as (t_1, b_1), (t_2, b_2) ... (t_m, b_m)

We get $\boxed{C + Dt_1 = b_1}$ $\boxed{C + Dt_2 = b_2}$ ... $\boxed{C + Dt_m = b_m}$

Put is matrix form
$$\begin{bmatrix} 1 & t_1 \\ 1 & t_2 \\ \vdots & \vdots \\ 1 & t_n \end{bmatrix} \begin{bmatrix} C \\ D \end{bmatrix} = \begin{bmatrix} b_1 \\ b_2 \\ \vdots \\ b_n \end{bmatrix} \quad \text{or} \quad Ax = b$$

The best solution $(\widehat{C}, \widehat{D})$ is the $\widehat{x}$ that minimizes the squared error E^2

$$E^2 = \|b - Ax\|^2 = (b_1 - C - Dt_1)^2 + \cdots + (b_m - C - Dt_m)^2$$

❖ Vector $p = A\widehat{x}$ is close as possible to b

❖ On the graph the error are the vertical distances b-C-Dt to the straight line (not perpendicular distances)

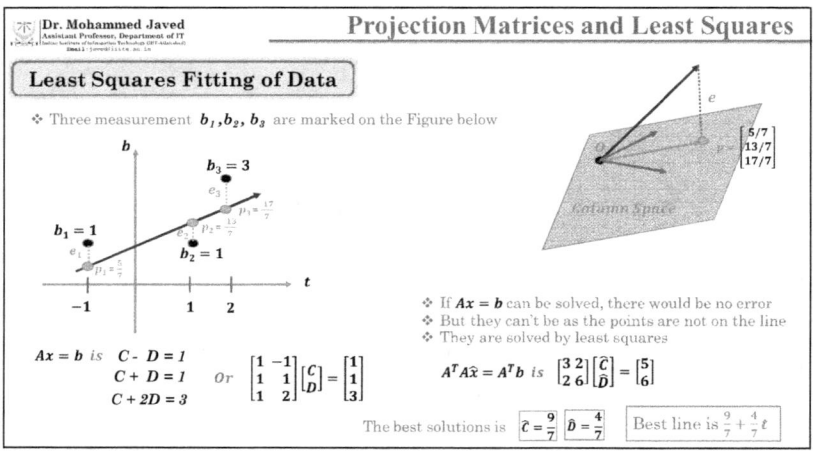

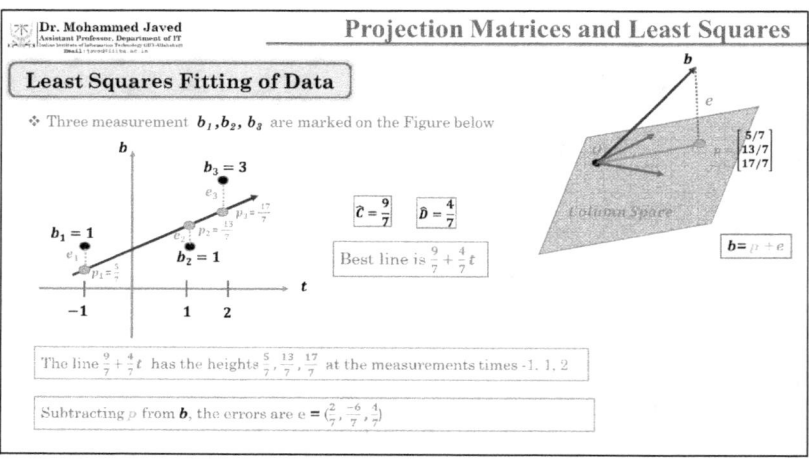

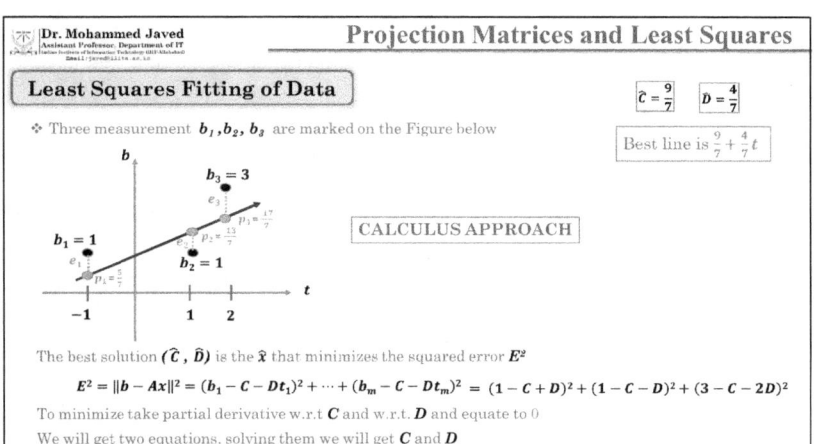

Dr. Mohammed Javed
Assistant Professor, Department of IT
[Indian Institute of Information Technology (IIIT-Allahabad)]
[Email: javed@iiita.ac.in]

Projection Matrices and Least Squares

Least Squares Fitting of Data

❖ Three measurement b_1, b_2, b_3 are marked on the Figure below

$$\hat{C} = \frac{9}{7} \qquad \hat{D} = \frac{4}{7}$$

Best line is $\frac{9}{7} + \frac{4}{7}t$

CALCULUS APPROACH

The best solution $(\hat{C}, \hat{D})$ is the $\hat{x}$ that minimizes the squared error E^2

$$E^2 = \|b - Ax\|^2 = (b_1 - C - Dt_1)^2 + \cdots + (b_m - C - Dt_m)^2 = (1 - C + D)^2 + (1 - C - D)^2 + (3 - C - 2D)^2$$

To minimize take partial derivative w.r.t C and w.r.t. D and equate to 0

We will get two equations, solving them we will get C and D

Dr. Mohammed Javed
Assistant Professor, Department of IT
[Indian Institute of Information Technology (IIIT-Allahabad)]
[Email: javed@iiita.ac.in]

Projection Matrices and Least Squares

Least Squares Fitting of Data

❖ Find a quadratic equation through the origin that is best fit for the points $(1,1)$, $(2,5)$, $(-1,-2)$

So our equation would be $ct + dt^2 = y$ which passes through the origin, so constant term is 0

$$A = \begin{bmatrix} 1 & 1 \\ 2 & 4 \\ -1 & 1 \end{bmatrix} \quad \hat{x} = \begin{bmatrix} c \\ d \end{bmatrix} \quad b = \begin{bmatrix} 1 \\ 5 \\ -2 \end{bmatrix} \qquad \text{We can't solve } A\hat{x} = b$$

We use $A^T A \hat{x} = A^T b$

$$A^T A = \begin{bmatrix} 1 & 2 & -1 \\ 1 & 4 & 1 \end{bmatrix} \begin{bmatrix} 1 & 1 \\ 2 & 4 \\ -1 & 1 \end{bmatrix} = \begin{bmatrix} 6 & 8 \\ 8 & 10 \end{bmatrix} \qquad A^T b = \begin{bmatrix} 1 & 2 & -1 \\ 1 & 4 & 1 \end{bmatrix} \begin{bmatrix} 1 \\ 5 \\ -2 \end{bmatrix} = \begin{bmatrix} 13 \\ 19 \end{bmatrix}$$

$$\begin{bmatrix} 6 & 8 \\ 8 & 10 \end{bmatrix} \hat{x} = \begin{bmatrix} 13 \\ 19 \end{bmatrix} \qquad D = \frac{-5}{2} \qquad C = \frac{11}{2} \qquad y = \frac{11}{2}t - \frac{-5}{2}t^2$$

Dr. Mohammed Javed
Assistant Professor, Department of IT
Indian Institute of Information Technology (IIIT) Allahabad
Email : javed@iiita.ac.in

Orthogonal Bases and Gram Schmidt

Orthogonal Basis

❖ In an orthogonal basis, every vector is perpendicular to every other vector

❖ In coordinate axes, they are mutually orthogonal

❖ Divide each vector by its length, to make it a unit vector

❖ That changes an orthogonal basis to an orthonormal basis

Formally, the vectors $q_1, \ldots, q_n$ are orthonormal if

$$q_i^T q_j = \begin{cases} 0 & \text{Whenever } i \neq j \quad \text{Giving the orthogonality} \\ 1 & \text{Whenever } i = j \quad \text{Giving the normalization} \end{cases}$$

❖ A Matrix with orthogonal columns will be called Q

❖ The most important example is the standard basis

❖ For x-y plane, the best known axes $e_1 = (1,0)$ and $e_2 = (0,1)$ are not only perpendicular but horizontal and vertical

❖ Q is here 2 by 2 Identity matrix

Dr. Mohammed Javed
Assistant Professor, Department of IT
Indian Institute of Information Technology (IIIT) Allahabad
Email : javed@iiita.ac.in

Orthogonal Bases and Gram Schmidt

Orthogonal Basis

❖ In n dimensions, the standard basis $e_1, \ldots, e_n$ again consists of the columns of $Q = I$

$$\text{Standard basis} \quad e_1 = \begin{bmatrix} 1 \\ 0 \\ 0 \\ \vdots \\ 0 \end{bmatrix}, \quad e_2 = \begin{bmatrix} 0 \\ 1 \\ 0 \\ \vdots \\ 0 \end{bmatrix}, \quad \ldots, \quad e_n = \begin{bmatrix} 0 \\ 0 \\ 0 \\ \vdots \\ 1 \end{bmatrix}$$

❖ If we have a subspace of $\mathbf{R}^m$, the stand vectors e_i might not lie in the subspace

❖ But the subspace always has an orthonormal basis,

❖ and it can be constructed in a simple way out of any basis

❖ This construction, which converts a skewed set of axes into a perpendicular set

❖ Is known as Gram-Schmidt Orthogonalization

$$\boxed{\textit{Leads to factorization } A = QR}$$

Dr. Mohammed Javed
Assistant Professor, Department of IT
Indian Institute of Information Technology (IIIT-Allahabad)
Email: javed@iiita.ac.in
Orthogonal Bases and Gram Schmidt

Orthogonal Basis

❖ An orthogonal matrix is a square matrix with orthonormal columns, then Q^T is Q^{-1}

❖ For square orthogonal matrices, the transpose is the inverse

Example: $Q = \begin{bmatrix} \cos\theta & -\sin\theta \\ \sin\theta & \cos\theta \end{bmatrix}$ $Q^T = Q^{-1} = \begin{bmatrix} \cos\theta & \sin\theta \\ -\sin\theta & \cos\theta \end{bmatrix}$

❖ The columns are orthogonal and also orthonormal because $\sin^2\theta + \cos^2\theta = 1$

❖ Any permutation matrix is an orthogonal matrix

❖ The columns are unit vectors and the transpose is the inverse

$$P = \begin{bmatrix} 0 & 1 & 0 \\ 0 & 0 & 1 \\ 1 & 0 & 0 \end{bmatrix} \quad Then \; P^{-1} = P^T = \begin{bmatrix} 0 & 0 & 1 \\ 1 & 0 & 0 \\ 0 & 1 & 0 \end{bmatrix}$$

Dr. Mohammed Javed
Assistant Professor, Department of IT
Indian Institute of Information Technology (IIIT-Allahabad)
Email: javed@iiita.ac.in
Orthogonal Bases and Gram Schmidt

Orthogonal Basis

❖ Suppose we project a point $b = (x, y, z)$ onto the x-y plane.

❖ Its projection is $p = (x, y, 0)$, and this is the sum of the separate projection onto the x and y axes

$$q_1 = \begin{bmatrix} 1 \\ 0 \\ 0 \end{bmatrix} \quad and \quad (q_1^T b)q_1 = \begin{bmatrix} x \\ 0 \\ 0 \end{bmatrix}$$

$$q_2 = \begin{bmatrix} 0 \\ 1 \\ 0 \end{bmatrix} \quad and \quad (q_2^T b)q_2 = \begin{bmatrix} 0 \\ y \\ 0 \end{bmatrix}$$

The overall projection matrix is

$$P = q_1 q_1^T + q_2 q_2^T = \begin{bmatrix} 1 & 0 & 0 \\ 0 & 1 & 0 \\ 0 & 0 & 0 \end{bmatrix} \quad and \quad P \begin{bmatrix} x \\ y \\ z \end{bmatrix} = \begin{bmatrix} x \\ y \\ 0 \end{bmatrix}$$

Projection onto a plane = sum of projections onto the orthonormal q_1 and q_2

 **Dr. Mohammed Javed**
Assistant Professor, Department of IT

Orthogonal Bases and Gram Schmidt

Orthogonal Basis

❖ When the measurement times averages to zero, fitting a straight line leads to orthogonal columns

❖ Take $t_1 = -3$, $t_2 = 0$ and $t_3 = 3$

❖ Then the attempt to fit $y = C + Dt$ leads to three equations in two unknowns

$$
\begin{aligned}
C + Dt_1 &= y_1 \\
C + Dt_2 &= y_2 \quad \text{Or} \\
C + Dt_3 &= y_3
\end{aligned}
\qquad
\begin{bmatrix} 1 & -3 \\ 1 & 0 \\ 1 & 3 \end{bmatrix}
\begin{bmatrix} C \\ D \end{bmatrix}
=
\begin{bmatrix} y_1 \\ y_2 \\ y_3 \end{bmatrix}
$$

❖ The columns $(1, 1, 1)$ and $(-3, 0, 3)$ are orthogonal

❖ We can project y separately onto teach column, the best coefficient $\hat{C}$ and $\hat{D}$ can be found separately

$$
\hat{C} = \frac{[1\ 1\ 1][y_1\ y_2\ y_3]^T}{1^2 + 1^2 + 1^2}
\qquad
\hat{D} = \frac{[-3\ 0\ 3][y_1\ y_2\ y_3]^T}{(-3)^2 + 0^2 + 3^2}
$$

❖ Notice that $\hat{C}$ is the mean of the data.
❖ $\hat{C}$ gives the best fit by a horizontal line.
❖ Whereas Dt is the best fit by straight line through the origin
❖ The columns are orthogonal,
❖ So the sum of these two separate pieces is the best fit by any straight line whatsoever.

Dr. Mohammed Javed
Assistant Professor, Department of IT

Orthogonal Bases and Gram Schmidt

Gram-Schmidt Process

❖ Suppose you are given three independent vectors a, b, c, and they orthonormal

❖ To project a vector v onto the first one, you compute $(a^T v)a$

❖ To project the same vector v onto the plane of the first two, you just add $(a^T v)a + (b^T v)b$

❖ To project onto the span of a, b, c you add three projections

❖ If they are not orthonormal, let us find a way to make them orthonormal

❖ We are given a, b, c and we want q_1, q_2, q_3

❖ There is no problem with q_1: it can go in the direction of a

❖ We divide by the length, so that $q_1 = \frac{a}{\|a\|}$ is a unit vector

❖ But q_2 should be orthogonal to q_1

❖ If second vector b has any component in the direction of q_1, that component has to subtracted

$$\text{Second vector } B = b - (q_1^T b)q_1 \qquad \text{and } q_2 = \frac{B}{\|B\|}$$

Dr. Mohammed Javed
Assistant Professor, Department of IT
Indian Institute of Information Technology (IIIT-Allahabad)
Email: javed@iiita.ac.in
Orthogonal Bases and Gram Schmidt

Gram-Schmidt Process

❖ We are given a, b, c and we want q_1, q_2, q_3

❖ There is no problem with q_1: it can go in the direction of a

❖ We divide by the length, so that $q_1 = \frac{a}{\|a\|}$ is a unit vector

❖ But q_2 should be orthogonal to q_1

❖ If second vector b has any component in the direction of q_1, that component has to subtracted

$$\text{Second vector } B = b - (q_1^T b)q_1 \qquad \text{and } q_2 = \frac{B}{\|B\|}$$

❖ The third orthogonal direction starts with vector c

❖ It will not be in the plane of q_1 and q_2, which is the plane of a and b

$$\text{Third vector } C = c - (q_1^T b)q_1 - (q_2^T b)q_2 \qquad \text{and } q_3 = \frac{c}{\|C\|}$$

This is the overall idea of Gram Schmidt, to subtract from every new vector its components in the directions that are already settled

---

Dr. Mohammed Javed
Assistant Professor, Department of IT
Indian Institute of Information Technology (IIIT-Allahabad)
Email: javed@iiita.ac.in
Orthogonal Bases and Gram Schmidt

Gram-Schmidt Process

❖ Suppose the independent vectors are a, b, c and we want q_1, q_2, q_3

$$a = \begin{bmatrix} 1 \\ 0 \\ 1 \end{bmatrix} \quad b = \begin{bmatrix} 1 \\ 0 \\ 0 \end{bmatrix} \quad c = \begin{bmatrix} 2 \\ 1 \\ 0 \end{bmatrix}$$

❖ To find q1, let us make the first vector into unit vector: $q_1 = \frac{a_1}{\sqrt{2}}$

$$\text{Second vector } B = b - (q_1^T b)q_1 = \begin{bmatrix} 1 \\ 0 \\ 0 \end{bmatrix} - \frac{1}{\sqrt{2}}\begin{bmatrix} 1/\sqrt{2} \\ 0 \\ 1/\sqrt{2} \end{bmatrix} = \frac{1}{2}\begin{bmatrix} 1 \\ 0 \\ -1 \end{bmatrix} \qquad \text{and } q_2 = \begin{bmatrix} 1/\sqrt{2} \\ 0 \\ -1/\sqrt{2} \end{bmatrix}$$

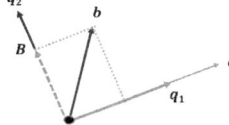

$$\text{Third vector } C = c - (q_1^T b)q_1 - (q_2^T b)q_2 = \begin{bmatrix} 2 \\ 1 \\ 0 \end{bmatrix} - \sqrt{2}\begin{bmatrix} 1/\sqrt{2} \\ 0 \\ 1/\sqrt{2} \end{bmatrix} - \sqrt{2}\begin{bmatrix} 1/\sqrt{2} \\ 0 \\ -1/\sqrt{2} \end{bmatrix} = \begin{bmatrix} 0 \\ 1 \\ 0 \end{bmatrix} \qquad \text{and } q_3 = \begin{bmatrix} 0 \\ 1 \\ 0 \end{bmatrix}$$

$$\text{Orthonormal Basis } Q = \begin{bmatrix} | & | & | \\ q_1 & q_2 & q_3 \\ | & | & | \end{bmatrix} = \begin{bmatrix} 1/\sqrt{2} & 1/\sqrt{2} & 0 \\ 0 & 0 & 1 \\ 1/\sqrt{2} & -1/\sqrt{2} & 0 \end{bmatrix}$$

Orthogonal Bases and Gram Schmidt

Dr. Mohammed Javed
Assistant Professor, Department of IT
Indian Institute of Information Technology (IIIT-Allahabad)
Email: javed@iiita.ac.in

Gram-Schmidt Process

❖ We started with independent vectors are a, b, c and ended with matrix Q with columns q_1, q_2, q_3

❖ The idea is to write the a's as combinations of the q's

❖ The vector b is a combination of the orthonormal q_1 and q_2

$$b = (q_1^T b)\, q_1 + (q_2^T b)\, q_2$$

❖ Similarly c is the sum of its q_1, q_2, q_3

$$c = (q_1^T c)\, q_1 + (q_2^T c)\, q_2 + (q_3^T c)\, q_3$$

QR Factors $\quad A = \begin{bmatrix} | & | & | \\ a & b & c \\ | & | & | \end{bmatrix} = \begin{bmatrix} | & | & | \\ q_1 & q_2 & q_3 \\ | & | & | \end{bmatrix} \begin{bmatrix} q_1^T a & q_1^T b & q_1^T c \\ & q_2^T b & q_2^T c \\ & & q_3^T c \end{bmatrix} = QR$

Positive Definite Matrices

Dr. Mohammed Javed

Assistant Professor, Department of IT
Indian Institute of Information Technology (IIIT-Allahabad)
Email: javed@iiita.ac.in

Video Lectures for the book contents are available at

https://www.youtube.com/channel/UCjuoLDHnvDBenbBdFD3pQUw

Content Reference Book :
Introduction to Linear Algebra by Gilbert Strang, MIT

Dr. Mohammed Javed
Assistant Professor, Department of IT
Email:javed@iiita.ac.in

Positive Definite Matrices

Background

❖ Every Symmetric matrix has real Eigenvalues

❖ Here we will learn methods that will guarantee that all those Eigenvalues are positive

❖ Based on three basic ideas – Pivots, Determinants, Eigenvalues

❖ The signs of Eigenvalues are very crucial

❖ For stability in differential equations, we needed negative Eigenvalues so that $e^{\lambda t}$ would decay

❖ The important problem through Science & Engineering and every problem of optimization

❖ Is to find the Minimum Point

❖ The mathematical problem is to move the second derivate test $F'' > 0$ into n dimensions

$$F(x,y) = 7 + 2(x+y)^2 - y \sin y - x^3$$ $$f(x,y) = 2x^2 + 4xy + y^2$$

Does $F(x,y)$ or $f(x,y)$ have a minimum at the point $x = y = 0$?

Dr. Mohammed Javed
Assistant Professor, Department of IT
Email:javed@iiita.ac.in

Positive Definite Matrices

Background $$F(x,y) = 7 + 2(x+y)^2 - y \sin y - x^3$$ $$f(x,y) = 2x^2 + 4xy + y^2$$

❖ The zero order terms $F(0,0) = 7$ and $f(0,0) = 0$ have no effect on the answer

❖ They simply raise or lower the graphs F and f

❖ The linear terms give a necessary condition:

❖ To have any chance of minimum, the first derivatives must vanish at $x = y = 0$

$$\frac{\partial F}{\partial x} = 4(x+y) - 3x^2 = 0 \quad \text{and} \quad \frac{\partial F}{\partial y} = 4(x+y) - y \cos y - y \sin y = 0$$

ALL ZERO

$$\frac{\partial f}{\partial x} = 4x + 4y = 0 \quad \text{and} \quad \frac{\partial f}{\partial y} = 4x + 2y = 0$$

❖ Thus $(x,y) = (0,0)$ is a stationary point for both the functions

❖ The surface $z = F(x,y)$ is a tangent to the horizontal plane $z = 7$,

❖ The surface $z = f(x,y)$ is tangent to the plane $z = 0$

❖ Question is whether the graphs go above those planes or not, as we move away from the tangency point $x = y = 0$

Dr. Mohammed Javed
Assistant Professor, Department of IT   **Positive Definite Matrices**

Background $F(x,y) = 7 + 2(x + y)^2 - y \sin y - x^3$ $f(x,y) = 2x^2 + 4xy + y^2$

❖ The Second derivatives at **(0,0)** are decisive:

$$\frac{\partial^2 F}{\partial x^2} = 4 - 6x = 4 \qquad\qquad \frac{\partial^2 f}{\partial x^2} = 4$$

$$\frac{\partial^2 F}{\partial x\,\partial y} = \frac{\partial^2 F}{\partial y\,\partial x} = 4 \qquad\qquad \frac{\partial^2 f}{\partial x\,\partial y} = \frac{\partial^2 f}{\partial y\,\partial x} = 4$$

$$\frac{\partial^2 F}{\partial x^2} = 4 + y \sin y - 2 \cos y = 2 \qquad\qquad \frac{\partial^2 f}{\partial x^2} = 2$$

❖ The two functions behave in exactly the same way near the origin
❖ **F** has a minimum if and only if **f** has a minimum
❖ The higher degree terms in F have no effect on the question of a local minimum
❖ But they can prevent it from being a global minimum

Dr. Mohammed Javed
Assistant Professor, Department of IT   **Positive Definite Matrices**

Background

❖ Every quadratic form $f = ax^2 + 2bxy + cy^2$ has a stationary point at the origin where

$$\frac{\partial f}{\partial x} = \frac{\partial f}{\partial x} = 0$$

❖ A local minimum would also be a global minimum
❖ The surface $z = f(x,y)$ will then be shaped like a bowl, resting on the origin
❖ If the stationary point of **F** is at $x = \alpha$ and $y = \beta$
❖ The only change would be to use the second derivative at α , β

Quadratic part of F

$$f(x,y) = \frac{x^2}{2}\frac{\partial^2 F}{\partial x^2}(\alpha,\beta) + xy\frac{\partial^2 F}{\partial x\,\partial y}(\alpha,\beta) + \frac{y^2}{2}\frac{\partial^2 F}{\partial y^2}(\alpha,\beta)$$

Dr. Mohammed Javed
Assistant Professor, Department of IT

Positive Definite Matrices

Background

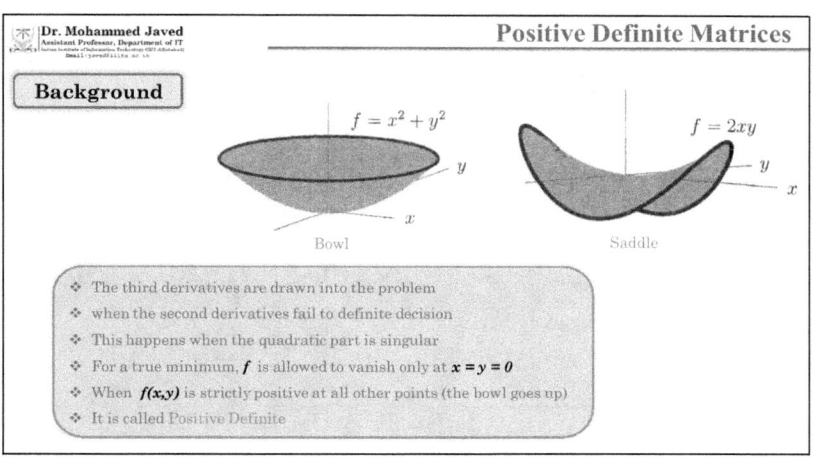

$f = x^2 + y^2$

$f = 2xy$

Bowl   Saddle

❖ The third derivatives are drawn into the problem
❖ when the second derivatives fail to definite decision
❖ This happens when the quadratic part is singular
❖ For a true minimum, f is allowed to vanish only at $x = y = 0$
❖ When $f(x,y)$ is strictly positive at all other points (the bowl goes up)
❖ It is called Positive Definite

Dr. Mohammed Javed
Assistant Professor, Department of IT

Positive Definite Matrices

Definite versus Indefinite: Bowl versus Saddle

❖ What condition on a, b, and c ensure that the quadratic $f(x, y) = ax^2 + 2bxy + cy^2$ is positive definite ?

❖ For a function with two variables, what is the correct replacement for the condition $\dfrac{\partial^2 F}{\partial x^2} > 0$

❖ Now we have three derivatives F_{xx} , $F_{xy} = F_{yx}$, F_{yy}

1. If $ax^2 + 2bxy + cy^2$ is positive definite, then necessarily $a > 0$
2. If $f(x, y)$ is positive definite, then necessarily $c > 0$
3. If $ax^2 + 2bxy + cy^2$ stays positive, then necessarily $ac > b^2$

Dr. Mohammed Javed
Assistant Professor, Department of IT

Positive Definite Matrices

Definite versus Indefinite: Bowl versus Saddle

Test for Minimum

$ax^2 + 2bxy + cy^2$ is positive definite, if and only if $a > 0$ and $ac > b^2$

Any $F(x, y)$ has a minimum at a point where $\frac{\partial F}{\partial x} = \frac{\partial F}{\partial y} = 0$ with

$$\frac{\partial^2 F}{\partial x^2} > 0 \quad \text{and} \quad \left[\frac{\partial^2 F}{\partial x^2}\right]\left[\frac{\partial^2 F}{\partial y^2}\right] > \left[\frac{\partial^2 F}{\partial x\, \partial y}\right]^2$$

Test for Minimum

❖ Since f has maximum whenever $-f$ has a minimum, we just reverse the sign of a, b, c

❖ Actually $ac > b^2$ unchanged

❖ The quadratic form is negative definite if and only if $a < 0$ and $ac > b^2$

❖ The same change applies for a maximum of $F(x,y)$

Dr. Mohammed Javed
Assistant Professor, Department of IT

Positive Definite Matrices

Definite versus Indefinite: Bowl versus Saddle

Singular Case $ac = b^2$

❖ We get positive semidfinite when $a > 0$

❖ We get negative semi definite when $a < 0$

❖ The prefix semi allows the possibility that f can equal zero, as it will be at the point $x = b$ and $y = -a$

❖ The surface $z = f(x,y)$ degenerates from a bowl into a valley

Saddle Point $ac < b^2$

❖ It happens when b dominates a and c

❖ It also occurs if a and c have opposite signs

❖ Then two directions give opposite results- one direction f increases, in the other it decreases

---

Dr. Mohammed Javed
Assistant Professor, Department of IT
Indian Institute of Information Technology (IIIT-Allahabad)
Email: javed@iiita.ac.in

Positive Definite Matrices

Linear Algebra Way

❖ The second derivative fits into a symmetric matrix

❖ The terms ax^2 and cy^2 appear in the diagonal

❖ The cross derivative $2bxy$ is split between the same entry b above and below

❖ A quadratic $f(x,y)$ comes directly from a symmetric 2 by 2 matrix

$$x^T A x \text{ in } \mathbb{R}^2 \qquad ax^2 + 2bxy + cy^2 \ = [x \ \ y]\begin{bmatrix} a & b \\ b & c \end{bmatrix}\begin{bmatrix} x \\ y \end{bmatrix}$$

❖ It generalizes immediately to n dimensions

❖ It is a perfect short hand for studying Maxima and Minima

❖ For any symmetric matrix A, the product $x^T A x$ is a pure quadratic form $f(x_1, \ldots, x_n)$

$$x^T A x \text{ in } \mathbb{R}^n \quad [x_1 \ \ x_2 \ \ . \ \ x_n]\begin{bmatrix} a_{11} & a_{12} & \cdot & a_{1n} \\ a_{21} & a_{22} & \cdot & a_{2n} \\ & & \cdot & \\ a_{n1} & a_{n2} & \cdot & a_{nn} \end{bmatrix}\begin{bmatrix} x_1 \\ x_2 \\ \cdot \\ x_n \end{bmatrix} = \sum_{i=1}^{n}\sum_{j=1}^{n} a_{ij}x_i x_j$$

Dr. Mohammed Javed
Assistant Professor, Department of IT
Indian Institute of Information Technology (IIIT-Allahabad)
Email: javed@iiita.ac.in

Positive Definite Matrices

Linear Algebra Way

Example: $f = 2x^2 + 4xy + y^2$ and $A = \begin{bmatrix} 2 & 2 \\ 2 & 1 \end{bmatrix}$ → Saddle Point

Example: $f = 2xy$ and $A = \begin{bmatrix} 0 & 1 \\ 1 & 0 \end{bmatrix}$ → Saddle Point

Example: A is 3 by 3 for $2x_1^2 - 2x_1 x_2 + 2x_2^2 - 2x_2 x_3 + 2x_3^2$

$$f = [x_1 \ \ x_2 \ \ x_3]\begin{bmatrix} 2 & -1 & 0 \\ -1 & 2 & -1 \\ 0 & -1 & 2 \end{bmatrix}\begin{bmatrix} x_1 \\ x_2 \\ x_3 \end{bmatrix} \to minimum \ at \ (0,0,0)$$

F has a minimum when the pure quadratic $x^T A x$ is positive definite

---

Dr. Mohammed Javed
Assistant Professor, Department of IT
Indian Institute of Information Technology (IIIT-Allahabad)
Email: javed@iiita.ac.in   **Positive Definite Matrices**

Tests for Positive Definiteness

❖ Following tests is a necessary and sufficient condition for the real
symmetric matrix A to be *Positive Definite*

1. $x^T A x > 0$ for all nonzero real vectors x
2. All the Eigenvalues of A satisfy $\lambda_i > 0$
3. All the upper left sub matrices A_k have positive determinants
4. All the pivots (without row exchanges) satisfy $d_k > 0$

$$\begin{bmatrix} 2 & -1 & 0 \\ -1 & 2 & -1 \\ 0 & -1 & 2 \end{bmatrix}$$ is a positive definite matrix

---

Minimum Principle

Dr. Mohammed Javed
Assistant Professor, Department of IT
Indian Institute of Information Technology (IIIT-Allahabad)
Email: javed@iiita.ac.in

Video Lectures for the book contents are available at

https://www.youtube.com/channel/UCjuoLDHnvDBenbBdFD3pQUw

Content Reference Book :
Introduction to Linear Algebra by Gilbert Strang, MIT

Linear Algebra Concepts with Real Life
Applications

Dr. Mohammed Javed
Assistant Professor, Department of IT
Indian Institute of Information Technology (IIIT-Allahabad)
Email: javed@iiita.ac.in

Minimum Principles

Quadratic Forms

❖ Let $x = \begin{bmatrix} x_1 \\ x_2 \end{bmatrix}$ Compute $x^T A x$ $A_1 = \begin{bmatrix} 4 & 0 \\ 0 & 3 \end{bmatrix}$ $A_2 = \begin{bmatrix} 3 & -2 \\ -2 & 7 \end{bmatrix}$

$$x^T A_1 x = [x_1 \quad x_2] \begin{bmatrix} 4 & 0 \\ 0 & 3 \end{bmatrix} \begin{bmatrix} x_1 \\ x_2 \end{bmatrix} = [x_1 \quad x_2] \begin{bmatrix} 4x_1 \\ 3x_2 \end{bmatrix} \boxed{= 4x_1^2 + 3x_2^2} \implies A_1 = \begin{bmatrix} 4 & 0 \\ 0 & 3 \end{bmatrix}$$

$$x^T A_2 x = [x_1 \quad x_2] \begin{bmatrix} 3 & -2 \\ -2 & 7 \end{bmatrix} \begin{bmatrix} x_1 \\ x_2 \end{bmatrix} = [x_1 \quad x_2] \begin{bmatrix} 3x_1 - 2x_2 \\ -2x_1 + 7x_2 \end{bmatrix}$$

$$= x_1(3x_1 - 2x_2) + x2(-2x_1 + 7x_2)$$

$$= 3x_1^2 - 2x_1x_2 - 2x_1x2 + 7x_2^2$$

$$\boxed{= 3x_1^2 - 4x_1x_2 + 7x_2^2} \implies A_2 = \begin{bmatrix} 3 & -2 \\ -2 & 7 \end{bmatrix}$$

Dr. Mohammed Javed
Assistant Professor, Department of IT
Indian Institute of Information Technology (IIIT-Allahabad)
Email: javed@iiita.ac.in

Minimum Principles

Foundation

❖ The heavy liquids sink to the bottom is a consequence of minimizing their potential energy

❖ When you sit on chair, sleep on a bed, the springs adjust themselves so that the energy is minimized

❖ These energies are nothing but **positive definite quadratic functions**

❖ The derivative of a quadratic is linear

❖ The first goal here to find the minimum principle that is equivalent to $Ax = b$, and

❖ The minimization equivalent to $Ax = \lambda x$

❖ We want to find the parabola $P(x)$ whose minimum occurs when $Ax = b$

The graph of $P(x) = \frac{1}{2} Ax^2 - bx$ has zero slope when $\frac{dP}{dx} = Ax - b = 0$

❖ This point a $x = A^{-1}b$ will be minimum if A is positive, the parabola opens upward

❖ To assure minimum of P(x), not a maximum or a saddle point, A should be Positive definite

Dr. Mohammed Javed
Assistant Professor, Department of IT

Minimum Principles

Foundation

If A is symmetric positive definite, then $P(x) = \frac{1}{2}x^T A x - x^T b$ reaches its minimum at the point where $A x = b$

At that point $P_{min} = -\frac{1}{2}b^T A^{-1} b$

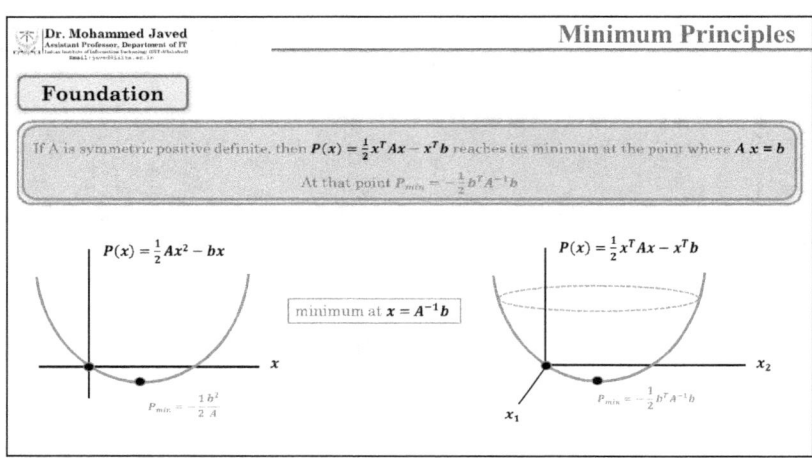

$P(x) = \frac{1}{2}Ax^2 - bx$

minimum at $x = A^{-1}b$

$P_{min} = \frac{1}{2}\frac{b^2}{A}$

$P(x) = \frac{1}{2}x^T A x - x^T b$

$P_{min} = -\frac{1}{2}b^T A^{-1}b$

x_1 x_2

Dr. Mohammed Javed
Assistant Professor, Department of IT

Minimum Principles

Illustration

Minimize $P(x) = x_1^2 - x_1 x_2 + x_2^2 - b_1 x_1 - b_2 x_2$ Set the partial derivative to zero. This gives $A x = b$

$$\frac{\partial P}{\partial x_1} = 2x_1 - x_2 - b_1 = 0$$

$$\frac{\partial P}{\partial x_2} = -x_1 + 2x_2 - b_2 = 0$$

$$\Rightarrow \begin{bmatrix} 2 & -1 \\ -1 & 2 \end{bmatrix} \begin{bmatrix} x_1 \\ x_2 \end{bmatrix} = \begin{bmatrix} b_1 \\ b_2 \end{bmatrix}$$

❖ Linear algebra recognizes this $P(x)$ as $\frac{1}{2}x^T A x - x^T b$

❖ And knows immediately that $Ax = b$ gives the minimum

❖ Substitute $x = A^{-1}b$ into $P(x)$

Minimum value at $P_{min} = \frac{1}{2}(A^{-1}b)^T A (A^{-1}b) - (A^{-1}b)^T b = -\frac{1}{2}b^T A^{-1}b$

❖ In applications, $\frac{1}{2}x^T A x$ is the internal energy and $-x^T b$ is the external work

❖ The system goes to $x = A^{-1}b$, where total energy $P(x)$ is minimum

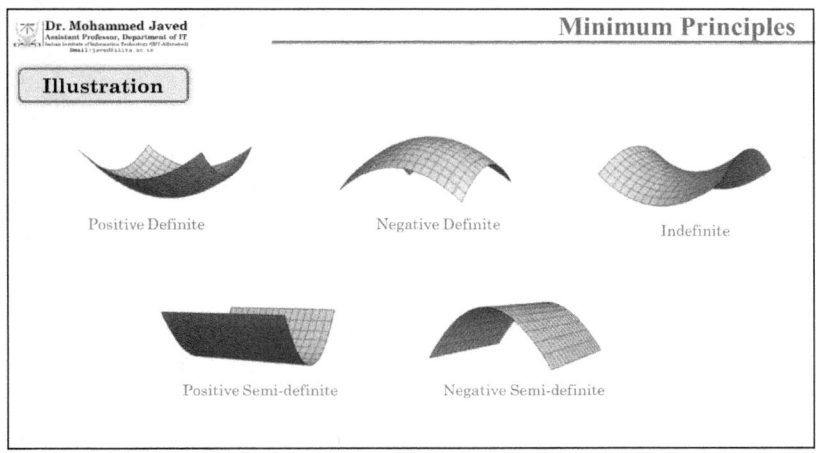

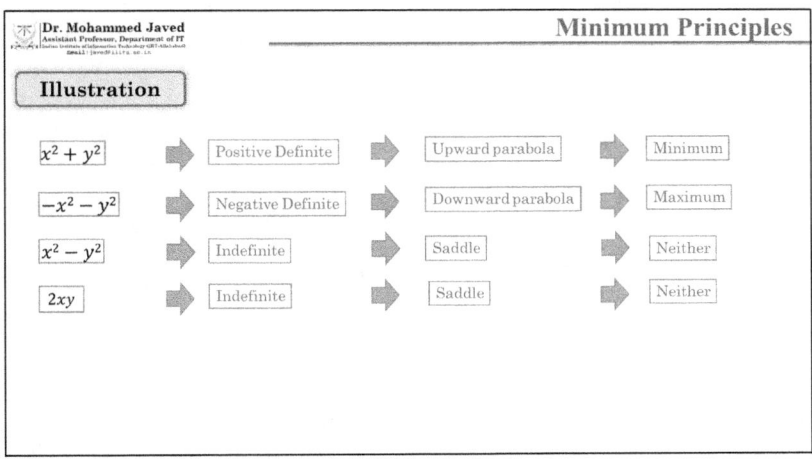

Dr. Mohammed Javed
Assistant Professor, Department of IT
Indian Institute of Information Technology (IIIT Allahabad)
Email: javed@iiita.ac.in

References

A. Gilbert Strang "Introduction to Linear Algebra", MIT
B. Google Images – www.google.com
C. Digital Image Processing by Gonzalez and Woods
D. https://www.mathsisfun.com/algebra/eigenvalue.html
E. www.geogebra.org
F. UCLA Math 33A
G. David C Lay "Linear Algebra and its Applications"

Dr. Mohammed Javed
Assistant Professor, Department of IT
Indian Institute of Information Technology (IIIT Allahabad)
Email: javed@iiita.ac.in

Thank You

www.ingramcontent.com/pod-product-compliance
Lightning Source LLC
Chambersburg PA
CBHW062250290526
45794CB00006B/2495